THE AFRICAN COOKBOOK

THE AFRICAN

COOKBOOK

BY BEA SANDLER

ILLUSTRATED BY DIANE AND LEO DILLON

A CITADEL PRESS BOOK   Published by Carol Publishing Group

Carol Publishing Group Edition - 1994

A Citadel Press Book
Published by Carol Publishing Group
Citadel Press is a registered trademark of Carol Communications, Inc.

Editorial Offices: 600 Madison Avenue, New York, NY 10022
Sales & Distribution Offices: 120 Enterprise Avenue, Secaucus, NJ 07094
In Canada: Canadian Manda Group, P.O. Box 920, Station U, Toronto,
Ontario, M8Z 5P9, Canada
Queries regarding rights and permissions should be addressed to:
Carol Publishing Group, 600 Madison Avenue, New York, NY 10022

Manufactured in the United States of America
ISBN 0-8065-1398-5 (pbk.)

12 11 10 9 8 7 6 5 4 3 2

Carol Publishing Group books are available at special discounts
for bulk purchases, sales promotions, fund raising, or
educational purposes. Special editions can also be created to
specifications. For details contact: Special Sales Department,
Carol Publishing Group, 120 Enterprise Ave., Secaucus, NJ 07094

Library of Congress Cataloging-in-Publication Data

Sandler, Bea.
   The African cookbook / Bea Sandler.
      p.   cm.
   "A Citadel Press book."
   Originally published : New York : World Pub. Co., 1970.
   1. Cookery, African. 2. Cookery—Africa. I. Title.
TX725.A4S28   1993
641.596—dc20   92-37570
                                      CIP

Acknowledgments

This book was compiled with the assistance, encouragement, and guidance of many people both in Africa and the U.S.A. The list is a long one, and my sincere thanks go to everyone on it, with my special gratitude to:

My lovely niece, Bonnie Kogos, who accompanied me on the African Food Safari, performed the necessary public relations, and acted as my editorial assistant.

Chef Kurt Linsi of the Ethiopian Airlines who contributed so much on Ethiopia and gave us some priceless food ideas. Also Miss Yeshi Taffesse of Ethiopian Airlines whose cook, Abeberich, helped us through the most difficult dishes of that country.

Mrs. Matilda Seya of Dar Es Salaam, Tanzania, at whose home we learned the art of cooking Duckling, Dar Es Salaam, and so many East African dishes. Also chef Jones Mayagola of Irinja, Tanzania.

Mrs. Ruth Habwe of Nairobi, Kenya, who prepared dishes of the Abaluhya tribe you'll find in this book; and Mrs. Phyllis Warden Ishmael, who demonstrated the Kikuyu dishes.

Mrs. Alberta A. Ollennu and her charming group of ladies who prepared and taught us to make the specialties of Ghana.

Mrs. Wilhemina Dukuly of Monrovia, at whose home a group of young dancers also participated in preparation of dishes Liberian; and Mrs. S. Spear who made us her fabulous Liberian Rice Bread and Coconut Pie.

Mamadou Lo and Henri Mercure with special thanks to his chef, Samba Camera, for "Senegalese Specialties," and the little lady whose name we did not get who runs the Djeddah Restaurant in Dakar.

Mrs. Umsalama Elshiekh of the Sudanese Mission and North Khartoum, Sudan, a young bride learned in the ways of cuisine of Sudan.

Chef Mohammed Taib of Casablanca, Morocco, who makes the "meanest" couscous we ever tasted, and superb Arab delicacies.

Mrs. Denise Rakotoniaina of the Mission of Malagasy and of Tananarive, Malagasy, whose dishes we adored, particularly the exciting uses of vanilla.

Mrs. Elizabeth Johnson of the South African Consulate for her help on the "Afrikaaner" segment of our book.

Mrs. Maria Theresa Castello Branco of the Portuguese Tourist Services and Mrs. Tina Johnson of Lourenço Marques, Mozambique, for the delightful ideas from Mozambique.

Mr. Stockbridge Bacchus, steward on Pan American World Airways, for his solicitude while we were aloft, his suggestions, and his help.

Additionally, for their untiring assistance in getting our book off the ground: Mrs. Patricia Calvert and Mr. Erich Kuehnert—Ethiopia; Miss Angela Christian, Ministry of Health of Ghana, Vivian Hammond, Patience Atiko Kotei, and Wilhemina Akwei—Ghana; Lorraine Saldanha, Mr. Ivor Davis, Public Relations—Kenya; Mr. and Mrs. James Thurber, Mr. Omar H. Al-Moody of the U.S. Information Service, and Mrs. G. Belcher—Tanzania; Mr. Bai T. Moore for permission to print his poem, Mr. T. Nelson Williams, and Miss Frances Caulker of Monrovia, Liberia.

To the women of Africa who graciously taught
us their ways of cooking and who have made
a genuine contribution to the culinary arts.

Foreword

Over the last few years there has been a tremendous growth of popular interest in Africa and its culture. Housewives are sewing with African fabrics which sell not only in the many new "Afro" shops but also in the big department stores. A whole generation, introduced to African music by Miriam Makeba, is fascinated with the "click" song. African playwrights like Wole Soyinka and novelists like James Ngugi and Chinua Achebe are studied in college literature courses. And recently in New York, moviegoers were able to see a Wolof-language film from the Cannes Festival by a Senegalese director.

Nevertheless, while African fashions, music, art, and literature have all become increasingly popular, African cuisine has remained almost unknown.

African cooking, like Africa itself, now embodies elements of several cultures—Arab, European, and Asian as well as black African. It is varied, it is interesting, and it is delicious. And food in Africa is perhaps more important in everyday social relations than it is in western cultures. African hospitality is without parallel anywhere else in the world. In many parts of Africa the arrival of a guest is followed almost automatically by the offering of food. It is an insult not to offer it, and, even if one is not hungry, it is an insult not to accept.

The recipes in this book are authentic, or as authentic as they need to be for American cooks. (Few readers will ever have to grind their own flour or prepare a goat from the hoof for the table.) The book itself is well organized and is full of useful suggestions. It has passed the scrutiny of the ladies on my staff, who like to cook, like to eat, and have been to Africa themselves.

Trusting their judgment and my own memories of the wonderful hospitality I have enjoyed in my travels to nearly every country south of the Sahara, I can heartily recommend this book to anyone with a taste for good food and a curiosity about this almost undiscovered facet of African culture.

Dr. James H. Robinson
Operation Crossroads Africa, Inc.

TABLE OF CONTENTS

Foreword by Dr. James H. Robinson   viii
Introduction   xiii
How to Use This Book   xvii

**Part I   Menus and Recipes from 11 African Countries
and the Island of Zanzibar**

Ethiopia   3
The Sudan   15
Morocco   25
Senegal   37
Kenya   47
Tanzania   57
Mozambique   67
Zanzibar   77
Malagasy   85
South Africa   95
Liberia   105
Ghana   115

Part II   An African Buffet   125

Part III   Additional Recipes

Appetizers   139
Soups   145
Fish   150
Poultry   162
Beef   171
Other Entrées   182
Starchy Accompaniments   185
Side Dishes and Relishes   192
Salads   197
Breads   204
Desserts   210
Beverages   222

Part IV   Appendix

All About Coconut   225
How to Prepare Butters   227
All About Greens   228
How to Cut Onions   229
Accompaniments for Curry   230
African Artifacts   231

Introduction

I first became interested in African cooking in 1964 when I was asked, as a menu consultant, to plan the meals for the Tree House Restaurants at the African Pavilion of the New York World's Fair. I accepted with much curiosity and some trepidation. Where to find recipes? Would they be good? Why were there, with the exception of couscous, no African dishes known to us?

A search in libraries, book stores, and consulate offices revealed that there has never been a book on African cooking published in the United States. We did find a few African books: an Ibo cookbook called *Yoruba Cookery, the Ghana Nutrition and Cookery Book,* and one from Nigeria called *What's to Eat?* These books proved amusing to read but hardly practical to follow. One book was prefaced with:

> In order to avoid confusion, the cigarette tin has been used as a unit of measurement, but the teacup can be used if preferred in place of the tin.

A couscous recipe was equally vague, calling for:

> Beans: *2 handfuls (in season); Cabbage: the heart of one; Saffron: a good pinch; Oil: a ladleful.*

These recipes were an interesting challenge and required much trial and error in our test kitchen!

In order to build up a collection of recipes, we invited Africans living in New York to bring us their recipes and cook for us. In this way we were able to observe their techniques and adapt them to methods which could be used by our chefs, as well as to experiment with spices and condiments so that the dishes could be enjoyed by Westerners. The results were marvelous! The Tree House Restaurants were enormously successful and among the most popular at the Fair. After repeated requests for recipes, we compiled the menus and recipes into a small book which was quickly sold out. Impressed by the enthusiasm and interest in African dishes on the part of so many people, I decided to go to Africa myself and broaden my knowledge of African cookery as well as add to my recipe collection. And so, in the spring of 1969, with my young niece Bonnie, I traveled through seven African countries visiting restaurants, homes, markets. Eating became a new experience!

We walked through the markets munching pastries and fruits, sampling the marvelous array of foods piled high, the scent of spices in the air. We ate, too, at the outdoor three-stone hearths where stews are served from earthen pots, kept at a simmer by the long-stick fires burning below. We sat cross-legged on mats and dipped into a common pot with the three fingers of our right hands as our host instructed. And we also had water poured over our hands into basins from elegant pitchers.

We found the African people everywhere friendly, interested, and more than generous with their time, patience, and help. AND we found superb cooking! Simple, direct dishes with new flavors and new combinations of foods. These dishes are not "haute cuisine," demanding hours if not days of complicated preparation, but fresh foods well prepared in an interesting variety of ways.

African cooking makes liberal use of food in its natural state and particularly those foods which "grow nearby." You will find in these recipes that many fruits and vegetables which we tend to use sparingly are called for in great abundance: fresh squash, pumpkin, carrots, bananas, sweet potatoes, mangos, papayas, coconuts, avocados. Melon, squash, and pumpkinseeds are dried and ground into flour with mortar and pestle. Ground peanuts are also used in many combinations of foods. Fish is freshly caught, home dried or smoked. Pulses (peas, beans, and lentils), almost forgotten in our cuisine, constitute an important part of the African diet.

The outstanding characteristic of much of African food is its spicy "hotness," achieved with an African pepper called *Pilli-pilli* (piri-piri in Mozambique and *Ber-beri* in Ethiopia) similar to, but stronger than, our cayenne pepper. Many visitors to Africa find the food inedible, when actually many dishes would have been enjoyed had the amount of pepper been adjusted to our Western palate. The climate is in large part responsible for the heavy consumption of their pepper, as it is considered to be a preventive medicine valuable in enabling the body to resist infection and disease. In parts of Africa the husband may judge how much his wife loves him by the amount of hot pepper she uses. If his food seems bland, he feels her ardor is "cooling."

In organizing this book we have taken eleven African countries and the Island of Zanzibar and devoted a chapter to each, presenting a complete menu with background information and serving suggestions. Thus each chapter contains:

An introduction to food and dishes of the country.

How the food is served to your "honored guest."

Suggestions on how you can present the menu.

A typical menu of the country.

A shopping list for a luncheon or dinner for eight people.

The recipes called for in these menus.

In Part II we have given recipes drawn from many countries arranged for an African buffet for twenty-five guests. In Part III we have assembled our collection of recipes, including those used in the Tree House Restaurants at the Fair. Finally, our Appendix gives some tips which I have garnered over the years; many are techniques and shortcuts in the handling of these foods.

Americans have become very sophisticated in their knowledge of foreign cuisines. Spanish, French, Chinese, Japanese, Hungarian, Italian restaurants abound, and we prepare and serve many of their dishes in our homes as a matter of course. The wonder is that African cuisine has remained virtually undercover for so long. We hope that this will serve as one of the beginning steps in a long and fruitful cross-cultural exchange. We invite you to discover, as we did, the delicacies and delights of African cooking!

NEW RICE AND DRY MEAT SOUP

by Bai T. Moore. Monrovia, Liberia

In October and November
All along the countryside
Paddy fields turn golden brown
And the chore of driving birds
Plus the other pests is ended.
Harvest time and all the joy
It brings with it drives hungry moons
Away leaving time for mirth and glee.
At harvest time I like the smell of
New country rice.
I like it steeped with kpleto leaves*
Young cocoa pods and okra
So each grain can stand alone.
New rice is good with dry meat soup
And preferably dry nyanga boy*
Plus other nyama,* such as
Billy goat pepper and bitter balls*
With a little nichlan oil* in it
To give it vitamin A, B, and C.

MR. MOORE is Under Secretary of the
Department of Information and Cultural Affairs
for the Liberian Government. He is also an
author and poet of note. His best known fiction
is "Murder in a Cassava Patch." His poetry
often appears in Liberian magazines and
other publications.

* **Kpleto leaves**—(the K is silent)—small green
   leaves—smaller than spinach.
* **Nyanga boy**—meat—usually venison.
* **Nyama nyama** means et cetera.
* **Bitter balls**—small eggplants.
* **Nichlan oil**—palm oil.

How To Use This Book

Most of the recipes yield eight portions but may be adjusted to serve any number. However, we would suggest that you prepare a larger quantity than you anticipate needing, as many of the recipes where foods are blended together taste even better on the second day.

Because African foods are spicy you will probably find that they will require more rice or other starch than you are accustomed to serving. When we prepared African dishes in our test kitchen we found that our guests usually helped themselves to several cups of rice despite the weight consciousness which generally prevails. Use your judgment in this matter keeping the following guides in mind.

1 cup raw rice yields 3½ to 4 cups cooked rice.
1 cup raw beans yields 4 cups cooked beans.
1 cup fine cereal yields 3 cups cooked cereal.

Cooking Terms for Action Recipes

For the first time you will probably be working with recipes that are "action-oriented." These recipes start with an action—the rest follows naturally in perfect "eye-flow" because your eye moves along with it. The "margin for error" is drastically reduced because you immediately understand the recipe as you read it. This technique is used by large restaurant chains to simplify food preparation and eliminate mistakes. Have you noticed lately how many package directions are being written in this style?

Recipes are designed to cut down on unnecessary wordage so you are, for example, directed to

Sauté   ½ cup   COARSELY CHOPPED ONIONS

To assure that you understand our *action* words (in case you do not already know them), these are the terms that will be used.

Baste pour cooking juices over foods while cooking to prevent drying out.

Beat mix ingredients vigorously with a spoon, beater, or whisk in a circular motion.

Blend work ingredients together into a thorough mixture.

Brush brush surface of food with liquid or semisoft fat.

Caramelize melt sugar over low heat to a gold-brown liquid.

Chill place in refrigerator and bring to 45° to 50°F.

Chop cut into small pieces.

Coat cover foods uniformly with breading (flour or crumbs).

Combine mix all ingredients together.

Cream work solid fat at room temperature to a soft, creamy consistency.

Cut In work in shortening by cutting into flour with two knives or pastry blender.

Dice cut food into cubes.

Drain pour off liquid through a sieve or colander.

Dredge coat heavily by dipping in seasoned flour.

Flake break flesh away from bones of fish in pieces.

Fold In gently mix by folding over; generally applied to beaten egg whites or whipped cream.

Grate shred by rubbing over a grater.

Grease coat a pan with fat or oil to prevent sticking.

Immerse completely cover with liquid.

Knead distribute the raising agent throughout dough by working with the heel of the hand.

Macerate stir fruits into juices or liqueurs to combine flavors.

Marinate stir foods into oil-and-vinegar, etc., combination to develop flavors.

Melt liquefy (fats) by heating.

Mince   chop as finely as possible.

Mix   combine ingredients so there is no separation.

Purée   sieve or mash to a smooth consistency.

Reduce   simmer to diminish in volume in order to concentrate flavor and thicken liquid.

Reserve   set aside for future use.

Roll Out   flatten dough with a rolling pin.

Roux, Make a   cook fat and flour until thick as a basis for sauce.

Score   make gashes with a knife without cutting entirely through.

Sift   pass through sifter or sieve to remove lumps.

Skewer   thread bits of food on a metal skewer or bamboo stick.

Slice   cut across food to desired thickness.

Stir   agitate in a circular motion with a spoon or fork, keeping food in motion.

Strain   pass foods through a strainer.

Toss   lift greens with a fork, combining them with dressing.

Whip   beat a liquid, as eggs or cream.

Cooking Methods

Bake   cook by dry heat in an oven.

Barbecue   cook over hot coals or fire.

Boil   cook above 212°F. on top of the stove in liquid.

Braise   brown quickly in fat, then cover and cook over low heat, cooking in its own juices or a small amount of liquid.

Broil   cook in close contact with flame or heat.

Brown   cook by frying or baking to obtain desired brown color.

Deep-Fat Fry   fry in fat deep enough to cover food being fried.

Dry Fry   brown without fat.

Fry   cook in oil or fat as directed.

Poach   cook in liquid just below boiling point.

Roast cook by dry heat to brownness; generally applied to meats.

Sear brown surface of meat quickly at high temperature.

Sauté shallow-fry in enough fat to cover bottom of pan.

Simmer cook foods just below boiling point with only occasional bubbles (from 185 to 212°F.).

Steam cook food with steam from boiling water (or gravy), food to be above the water.

Stew simmer slowly, covered, to thick consistency.

Correct the Seasoning means adding the YOU ingredient. The most important ingredient in any recipe is YOU—the eye that does the measuring, the hand that does the blending, adds the seasoning, and the garnish—YOU add that special touch, the flair that makes any recipe your own creation. The YOU ingredient is the key to your success. Use it wisely.

Your Larder

African foods are hot and spicy. Be sure to have the following spices and condiments on hand, as they will not be included in the market lists.

Allspice, whole and ground	crystallized	Pepper
Bay Leaves, whole dried	Lemon Peel, grated	Black, peppercorns, coarse and ground
Cardemom, ground	Monosodium Glutamate	Cayenne (red)
Chili	Mace, ground	Crushed Red
Chili Powder	Mustard, prepared and dry (English)	Saffron
Cinnamon, powdered	Nutmeg, ground	Salt, coarse (Kosher) and regular
Cloves, whole and powdered	Onion, salt and powdered	Sesame Seeds
Cumin, ground or whole	Orange Peel, grated	Thyme
Curry Powder	Oregano	Turmeric
Garlic Powder	Paprika	Vanilla
Ginger, powdered and	Parsley, dried	

Also have on hand the following staples, as these also are not included on the market lists.

Baking Powder	Flour	Sugar, white and brown
Baking Soda	Oil, vegetable and olive	Vinegar, white and cider
Cornstarch		

PART I

MENUS AND RECIPES FROM
11 AFRICAN COUNTRIES
AND THE ISLAND OF ZANZIBAR

Ethiopia

This ancient country, old even before the time of Christ, is called the land of thirteen months of sunshine, (the Ethiopian calendar having twelve months of thirty days and an extra month of five days called Pagume). The climate is balmy and pleasant with rain falling rarely except in the summer months.

Here, where the Queen of Sheba once ruled, primitive and modern cultures exist side by side. In the villages, families live in "tukels" made of stone with thatched roofs, and life goes on today much as it has for centuries. In Addis Ababa, there are new white buildings of reinforced concrete in the midst of bustling, energetic people. Women with exquisite facial bone structure wear *shamas,* a gauzelike white fabric covering them from head to foot. Men wear either Ethiopian robes or Western dress.

The open-air market of Addis is the largest and most exciting in all of Africa. The market seems to stretch for miles. Everything is on display, from clothing and household wares to treadle sewing machines. And the food! Women sit cross-legged on the ground with tiny scales to measure spices for the *Wat*—the stews cooked in every home. Grains, called *Tef,* in huge bags are ready for the housewives who make *Injera*—the unleavened bread prepared today as it was a thousand years ago. The low stands are heaped with citrus fruits, bananas, grapes, pomegranates, figs, custard apples (a delectable tropical fruit), and vegetables of all kinds, including the wonderful red onion of this area and *Gommen,* a kale-like plant used in the *Alechi:* the stews of the fast days. The meats on sale are beef, lamb, and goat. You'll find a sort of rancid butter cut from a large block and sold in chunks wrapped in wax paper, along with *Iab,* a soft cheese wrapped and kept cool in banana leaves.

The Coptic Church, the dominant religious sect in Ethiopia since the fourth century, dictates many food customs. There are fast days when meat is prohibited and pulses—lentils, peas, field peas, chick peas, and peanuts—are used in making the *Wat* and *Alechi.* No one is permitted to eat pork. The hand-washing ceremony before and after meals is a religious ritual. Even the manner in which meats are prepared is dictated.

The hottest, most peppery food in all of Africa is found in Ethiopia. The foreigner, not accustomed to the hot spice *Ber-beri* or *Awaze,* specially prepared with red pepper and containing as many as fifteen spices, cannot take it. But if you cut down on the pepper, you will find the food to be as interesting and exciting as anything you have ever eaten.

How a Dinner Is Served in Ethiopia

A meal in Ethiopia is an experience. When you have dinner in an Ethiopian home or restaurant, you eat the tablecloth!

One or two of the guests are seated on a low comfortable divan and a *mesab,* a handmade wicker hourglass-shaped table with a designed domed cover is set before them. The other guests are then seated round the table on stools about eight inches high covered with monkey fur.

A tall, stunning woman with characteristically high cheekbones and soft skin, dressed in a *shama,* carries a long-spouted copper ewer or pitcher in her right hand, a copper basin (which looks like a spitoon) in her left hand, and a towel over her left arm. She pours warm water over the fingers of your right hand, holding the basin to catch the excess, and you wipe your hands on the towel that hangs over her arm.

The *mesab* is taken out of the room and returned shortly with the domed cover. She removes the dome and the table is covered with what looks like a gray cloth overlapping the edge of a huge tray. But it is not a "tablecloth" at all. It is the *Injera,* the sourdough pancake-like bread of Ethiopia. Food is brought to the table in enamel bowls and portioned out on the "tablecloth!" When the entire *Injera* is covered with an assortment of stews, etc., you tear off a piece about two or three inches square and use this to "roll" the food in—the same way you would roll a huge cigarette. Then just swoop it up and pop it into your mouth. Your host might "pop" the first little "roll" in your mouth for you. It takes a bit of doing to accomplish this feat but once you master it, you cannot help enjoy it.

Our server returns with individual long-necked bottles from which you drink *Tej,* an amber-colored honey wine. It is put on a little table close by. Or she may bring a weakly carbonated water or *Tella,* the homemade beer.

You learn that you are eating Chicken *Wat* and Lamb *Wat*—two peppery stews; *lab*—cottage cheese and yogurt with special herbs giving it an acidic lemon flavor; and *Kitfo*—ground raw beef, which we are told is considered the dessert of the meal.

No other dessert is served. Coffee comes in on a tray in tiny Japanese cups served black with sugar.

Dinner is concluded with hand-washing again and incense is burned.

How You Can Present an Ethiopian Dinner

You'll need the largest Teflon skillet you can find and a high round tray, at least fifteen inches in diameter.

It would be impossible to make *Injera,* the pancake which serves as a "tablecloth," for it is made in Ethiopia with *Tef,* a flour not available here. The closest substitute devised in our test kitchen is a large buckwheat pancake which does not taste exactly like *Injera* but is similar in texture and color. (You will like the buckwheat pancake more than the actual *Injera.*)

Make four or five 9- to 10-inch pancakes as the recipe directs and overlap them on the 15-inch tray to look like a "tablecloth," letting the outer edges overlap the tray. Place the tray on a bridge table or a small round table around which your guests are crowded side by side on bridge chairs or stools. (If you prefer you can use a low coffee table with small stools all around and have two or three of your guests sit on the sofa.) Conduct the hand-washing ceremony as described earlier before you serve the meal.

The tray containing the large pancakes should be covered with aluminum foil. Remove the foil when the tray is placed on the table.

Bring in the bowls of *Wat,* one at a time. Ladle out right on the *Injera* one portion of *Doro* (chicken) *Wat* and one hard-boiled egg to each guest —then serve the Lamb *Wat,* the *lab* (a cottage cheese and yogurt mixture), and the *Kitfo* until the *Injera* is covered with individual portions of food. Everyone eats from the tray but has his part of the dinner in front of him.

Keep folding tables handy at easy access to each guest for his beverage —*Tella* (beer) or just plain carbonated water. If you can find attractive decanters with round bottoms, small enough for one cup, it might be fun to serve the honey wine to each guest in this manner. He would then drink it right from the bottle.

Provide forks for the uninitiated who may give up before they learn to eat in the traditional way. One important warning when using buckwheat *Injera;* the stews should be thick enough so that they do not soak through the pancake.

When the food and the *Injera* "tablecloth" are completely consumed, dinner is over.

Coffee in demitasse cups is served right after dinner. Later, much later, you can serve slices of fresh pineapple or melon, and *Dabo Kolo,* the tiny, fried, snacklike cookies so popular in Ethiopia.

Menu from Ethiopia

INJERA
Bread of Ethiopia

SEGA WAT
Lamb Dices

DORO WAT
Chicken Stew
with Hard-Boiled Eggs

IAB
Cottage Cheese and
Yogurt

KITFO
Tartar Steak

or

TEJ
Honey Wine

DABO KOLO
Fried Cookies

TELLA
Beer

Shopping List for Eight

Meats, poultry
1 3-lb. chicken
2 lbs. lamb from leg
1 lb. freshly ground
    lean beef
½ lb. pepperoni

Dairy
1 lb. cottage cheese
½ pt. yogurt
1 dozen eggs
½ lb. butter

Fruits and Vegetables
1 bunch parsley
2 lemons
3 lbs. onions
1-2 melons or seasonal
    fruit for dessert
1½ lbs. tomatoes

Beverages
1 bottle white wine
    such as Riesling or
    Soave

Groceries
1 box biscuit mix
1 box buckwheat pan-
    cake flour
1 pint olive oil
1 lb. honey
1 dozen cans mild beer
2 large bottles soda
    water
1 bottle ketchup

INJERA | Bread

This unleavened bread of Ethiopia is really a huge pancake made by the women in special large pans with heavy covers. The *Tef* batter is saved from an earlier baking and added to the new batter to give it a sourdough quality. It is poured at a thin consistency and baked covered so that the bottom of the pancake does not brown. The top should be full of air holes before the pancake is covered. The heavy cover steams the pancake so that when it is finished it looks like a huge thin rubber sponge. Since *Tef* is not available here, we had to find a way to simulate *Injera* in our test kitchen. The combination of buckwheat flour mix and biscuit mix seems to produce the closest substitute. Making it is easy, but getting the *Injera* texture takes a bit of experimentation, first, because not all pancake mixes are alike and secondly, it is important to cook the pancake at just the right temperature. This takes a bit of practice.

Yield: 5 9-inch pancakes

Combine	1 cup	BUCKWHEAT PANCAKE MIX
	1 cup	BISCUIT MIX
	1	EGG
Add	1 Tbs.	OIL
	1½-2 cups	WATER to obtain an easy pouring consistency.

Bring a 10-inch skillet or a handled griddle pan to medium heat uniformly over the flame. Do not let the pan get too hot.

Spread ½ tsp. OIL over the pan with a brush.

Fill a measuring cup (with spout) or a large cream pitcher with batter.

Pour the mixture on the hot pan or griddle in a thin stream starting from the *outside* and going in circles to the center from left to right. As soon as it bubbles uniformly all over remove from heat. Pancakes should be 9 inches in diameter.

Place the pan in an oven at 325° for about 1 minute until the top is dry but not brown.

Arrange the five pancakes overlapping each other so as to completely cover a fifteen-inch tray, thus forming the *Injera* "tablecloth."

IAB | Cottage Cheese and Yogurt

Iab is a white curd cheese very much like the Greek *feta*. Special herbs are added (and sometimes chopped vegetables) which give it its characteristically acid taste. Since the cheese used in Ethiopia is not available here, this recipe is an attempt to simulate *Iab*.

Yield: 1 quart

In a 1-quart bowl:

Combine		
1 lb.	SMALL-CURD COTTAGE CHEESE or FARMER CHEESE
4 Tbs.	YOGURT
1 Tbs.	GRATED LEMON RIND
1 tsp.	SALAD HERBS
2 Tbs.	CHOPPED PARSLEY
1 tsp.	SALT
¼ tsp.	BLACK PEPPER.

The mixture should be moist enough to spoon but dry enough to stay firm when served. Drain off excess liquid. One or two heaping tablespoons of *Iab* is placed on the *Injera* before each guest.

TEJ | Honey Wine

Tej is the Ethiopian wine made from "honey raw with comb" cooked with hops (*Gesho*), and it takes a special talent to make it. We simulated *Tej* for our Ethiopian dinner as follows:

Yield: approximately 1 quart

Combine		
1 pint	WHITE WINE, light, neither dry nor sweet.
1 pint	WATER
4 Tbs.	HONEY.

Chill and serve in ½-cup decanters or wine glasses. Be sure it is very cold. Whatever white wine you use should not have strong characteristic taste of its own. A mild white wine of the Soave or Riesling type thinned with water and to which honey is added is as close to *Tej* as one can get without going through the fermentation process. (You may be able to find honey wine ready to use. Ask at your local liquor store. If not available proceed as above.)

DORO WAT | Chicken Stew

In Ethiopia, about 4 tablespoons of *Ber-beri,* Ethiopian red pepper, is used in each recipe. It is extremely hot. In our adaptation, we use cayenne pepper and paprika (which is not Ethiopian) to bring it to the characteristic dark color and flavor. Even cayenne pepper should be used sparingly.

Yield: 8 portions

In a 4- to 6-quart Dutch oven or heavy stewpot:

Brown	3 cups	BERMUDA ONION chopped finely, *without fat,* until quite dark, stirring constantly.
Add	3 oz.	BUTTER or OLIVE OIL
	½ tsp.	CAYENNE PEPPER
	1 tsp.	PAPRIKA
	½ tsp.	BLACK PEPPER
	¼ tsp.	GINGER.
Blend	the seasonings into the onions.	
Add	1 cup	WATER.
Soak	1 3-lb.	CHICKEN cut in 1-inch pieces, bones left on and including neck and gizzards, in
	2 cups	WATER to which
	¼ cup	LEMON JUICE has been added, for 10 minutes.
Drain	the water from each piece of chicken.	
Add	chicken to onion mixture, stirring it through. Cover.	
Simmer	over low heat until chicken is tender.	
Add	more water, if necessary, to bring to stew texture (or if *Wat* is watery, thicken with 2 tablespoons of flour dissolved in 2 tablespoons of water).	
Add	8	PEELED HARD-BOILED EGGS a few minutes before serving.

SEGA WAT | Ethiopian Lamb

Proceed as above but use 2 lbs. of lamb (from leg) instead of chicken and only 1 cup of chopped onions. The lamb is cut in ½-inch cubes, the water is not added, and the lamb is sautéed on all sides until quite dry and well done.

KITFO | Ethiopian Tartar Steak

Chopped beef should be freshly ground just before serving. It is served raw.

Yield: 8 portions

In a 9-inch skillet:

Melt	2 oz.	BUTTER.
Add	¼ tsp.	CAYENNE PEPPER
	¼ tsp.	CHILI PEPPER
	1 tsp.	SALT and stir through thoroughly.
Add	1½ lbs.	LEAN ROUND STEAK, freshly ground,
Mix	thoroughly. Serve immediately. Do not cook.	

If your guests prefer the *Kitfo* cooked, sauté it over low heat for about 5 minutes, stirring constantly.

CHEF KURT LINSI'S QUEEN OF SHEBA SALAD

Chef Linsi serves this salad when he prepares an Ethiopian dinner, as he feels that a salad is lacking in the Ethiopian presentation. It's pretty hot too, so be careful with the hot-pepper sauce and hot chilies.

Yield: 8 small salads

In a 1-quart bowl:

Combine	1½ lbs.	FIRM TOMATOES, cut in tiny wedges with seeds removed
	½ cup	SWEET ONIONS, finely chopped
	1 clove	GARLIC, finely chopped
	1	HOT CHILI PEPPER, finely chopped
	½ cup	PEPPERONI, thinly sliced (optional).

Sheba Sauce

Combine	1 cup	KETCHUP
	¼ cup	VINEGAR
	½ cup	OIL
	½ cup	SWEET WHITE WINE (Muscatel or Madeira)
	1 tsp.	WORCESTERSHIRE SAUCE
	1 tsp.	SALT

¼ tsp.   BLACK PEPPER
few drops TABASCO SAUCE.

Marinate the tomato mixture in the sauce. Serve in sauce dishes without lettuce or drain well and place in the center of the *Injera*.

DABO KOLO | Little Fried Snacks

They will look like flat peanuts, and are served as a snack or with cocktails; and like peanuts, once you start eating them you can't stop.

In a 1-quart bowl:

Mix   2 cups   ALL-PURPOSE FLOUR
½ tsp.   SALT
2 Tbs.   SUGAR
½ tsp.   CAYENNE PEPPER
¼ cup   OIL.

Knead together and add WATER, spoonful by spoonful, to form a stiff dough.

Knead dough for 5 minutes longer.

Tear off a piece the size of a golf ball.

Roll it out with palms of hands on a lightly floured board into a long strip ½ inch thick.

Snip into ½-inch pieces with scissors.

Spread about a handful of the pieces on an ungreased 9-inch frying pan (or enough to cover bottom of pan). Cook over heat until uniformly light brown on all sides, stirring up once in a while as you go along. Continue until all are light brown.

VEGETABLE ALECHA | Vegetable Stew

The Copts in Ethiopia have many fast days on which they are not permitted to eat meat. Vegetables *Alechas* and *Wats* are substituted on these days. (The *Wat* differs from the *Alecha* in that it is made with a spice called *Ber-beri* or *Awaze*.)

Yield: 8 portions

In a 4-quart saucepan:

Sauté	1 cup	BERMUDA ONIONS in
	4 Tbs.	OIL
		until soft but not brown.
Add	4	CARROTS, peeled and cut in 1-inch slices
	4	GREEN PEPPERS, cleaned and cut in quarters
	3 cups	WATER
	1 6-oz. can	TOMATO SAUCE
	2 tsp.	SALT
	½ tsp.	GROUND GINGER.
Cook	for 10 minutes covered.	
Add	4	POTATOES cut in thick slices.
Plunge	2	TOMATOES in boiling water, remove skins, cut in 8 wedges each, and add to stew.
Cover	and cook for 10 minutes.	
Add	8	CABBAGE WEDGES, 1 inch wide.
Sprinkle	with SALT and PEPPER.	
Cook	until vegetables are tender.	
Correct the Seasoning		
Place	in an attractive bowl and portion out uniformly.	

The Sudan

The Sudan is Africa in microcosm: a large country with geographic extremes ranging from sandy desert to tropical forest. It is culturally a loose association of almost 600 tribes who have Arabic as their common language. The French, the English, and the Italians have all had colonies in the Sudan. The cuisine is a melding of the many varied backgrounds of the peoples who have influenced its history.

The ritual of hospitality is as important in the Sudan as it is in other Arab countries. And while there is a measure of similarity in all the Arab countries, each has its unique characteristics. For example, no other country prepares coffee as the Sudanese do, and if this country acquired culinary fame, it is for its *Jebena Sudanese.* The Sudanese fry their coffee beans in a special pot over charcoal and then grind it with cloves and certain spices. They steep it in hot water and serve it lovingly in tiny coffee cups after straining it through a special fresh grass sieve.

In Sudan, if you are an important guest, a sheep will be slaughtered in your honor. Many dishes will then be prepared, each more delicious than the last.

Favorite meats are lamb and chicken. Rice is the staple starch. Breads are the Arabian *Khudz,* but the Sudanese also make *Kisra,* an omelette-like pancake which is part of the Sudanese dinner. Vegetables, fresh and cooked, are of infinite variety. The okra, which incidentally came to the United States from Africa, is an important ingredient in a *Bania-Bamia,* an okra-lamb stew. You must try *Maschi,* a triple tomato dish stuffed with beef, as it is such fun to make.

As in most Arabic countries, fruits are peeled and cut in small slices for dessert, but the Sudanese also love sweets and every housewife knows how to make *Creme Caramela* (page 22).

You will like their unusual teas which can be made quite simply. But if you prefer to serve coffee, make it a demitasse.

How a Dinner Is Served in the Sudan

The concern and respect shown to one's guest throughout Africa, and from which we can learn much, is no greater anywhere than in the Sudan. As a guest enters a Sudanese home, he is immediately offered *Abre* or *Tabrihana,* a refreshing nonalcoholic fruit drink only slightly sweetened so as not to dull the appetite. This is a symbolic gesture welcoming him after his "long journey."

Dinner is served on a low table and guests are made comfortable on pillows decorated with ostrich feathers. The table is bare.

The Arabic custom of pouring water over the hands of the guests from the *Ebrig,* a handsome shiny copper ewer (pitcher), and catching the water into an equally handsome copper basin is an important ritual in the Sudan. Each guest is offered a towel with which to wipe his hands.

Large cloths to cover the knees are given to each guest in place of napkins.

Upon the signal of the host, dinner is served. It starts with soup, brought out in individual bowls on a huge, round, decorated copper tray. The large tray is placed on the table. Spoons are offered to the guests.

After the soup has been enjoyed, the entire tray is removed and a second larger tray is brought in with all the dishes of the main course resting on beaded doilies made by the women. There may be five or six dishes to dip into. (No knives or forks are used but spoons may be provided.) But most of the Sudanese eat the main course from common dishes using *Kisra* or *Khupz* (their great flat breads) to sop up the mixtures. Four dishes are individually served—the soup, the salad, the *Shata* (red-hot spice) and the dessert.

When the entrée is served, small plates or bowls are also brought in from which the host or hostess dishes out portions of salad and gives each guest a spoon with which to eat the salad. Again hands are washed and everyone looks forward to dessert. Sweets like *Creme Caramela* are usually served and are preferred to fruits. No beverage is served with dinner but one may ask for water. After dinner everyone relaxes and enjoys the famous *Guhwah,* coffee served from the *Jebena,* the stunning little coffee-pot from which it is poured into tiny cups. If tea is preferred, the succulent spiced teas with cloves or cinnamon are served. Finally an incense burner filled with sandalwood is placed in the center of the room, a touch leaving the guests with a feeling of delightful relaxation.

How You Can Present a Dinner from Sudan

Use a low table, perhaps in the living room, and place cushions on the floor around it. Remind your guests to be comfortably clad if you plan to serve dinner in this way. Use a plain cloth on the table and, instead of a centerpiece, place flowers around the room. The table should be bare. Give your guests large cloths to cover their knees instead of napkins.

Have a pitcher of cold orange or grapefruit juice on hand and offer each guest a small glass filled with juice as he arrives.

You will need large trays on which to serve the meal. On the largest tray place a small bowl of soup, *Shorba,* for each guest and pass the spoons separately. The guest holds the bowl in his left hand as he eats and, when he is finished, returns the empty bowl to the tray. The entire tray is then removed.

Use the second largest tray for the platter of *Maschi,* a two-quart bowl of white rice, a stack of eight *Kisra* (bread), a bowl of *Salata* and individual tiny dishes of *Shata,* the hot spice which each guest uses to his taste. If there is room on the tray, there should be a stack of little plates or small salad bowls. The hostess may serve individual salads or guests may help themselves.

If your guests are too squeamish to sop up the dinner with the *Kisra,* give them each a small dinner plate with a fork and teaspoon and ask them to take a portion of *Maschi* and rice. Water glasses should be available on a small side table but do not serve water unless it is requested. When the guests have finished eating, the plates are put back on the tray and the tray removed.

On the third tray serve a platter of shimmering *Creme Caramela* beautifully decorated with candied cherries and a compote dish and a spoon for each guest.

A small tray bearing a teapot and tea cups (each holding a small piece of stick cinnamon) and an open bowl of sugar is brought in last.

This is the time to light your incense burner and fill the room with the delicate fragrance of sandalwood.

Menu from the Sudan

SHORBA
Purée of Lamb
Khartoum

ROUZ MALFULFEL
White Rice

MASCHI
Tomatoes Stuffed with
Chopped Beef

SALATA MI JIBNA
Salad with Oriental
Cheese

SHATA
Hot Spice

KISRA
Bread of the Sudan

CREME CARAMELA

CINNAMON TEA

Shopping List for Eight

Meat
3 lbs. lamb bones
2 lbs. chopped beef

Specialty Items
In gourmet or middle
Eastern shop:
1 pkg. Middle Eastern
flat bread
½ lb. grated Oriental or
Parmesan cheese
1 lb. English tea
1 bottle banana extract
or vanilla

Dairy
1 container plain yogurt
1 qt. milk
1 dozen eggs
½ lb. butter

Fruit and Vegetables
2 lbs. onions
1 bunch carrots
1 large cabbage
½ lb. string beans
1 head garlic
3 lemons
8 large firm tomatoes
4 medium tomatoes
fresh dill

Groceries
½ pint peanut butter
2 lbs. white rice
2 6-oz. cans tomato
paste
1 large jar green olives
1 jar maraschino or
candied cherries
½ pt. bottled lemon
juice
1 package stick cinna-
mon

SHORBA | Purée of Lamb Khartoum

This is a most interesting soup. It is a medium purée sparkled with peanut butter and lemon. The Sudanese usually add rice but it is omitted here since rice is served with the entrée. Three cloves of garlic may be a bit strong so start with one clove and test the soup as it cooks to see if you would prefer a more penetrating garlic flavor.

Yield: 2 quarts of soup (8 1-cup portions)

	In a 6-quart saucepan:	
Simmer	3 lbs.	LAMB BONES in
	2 quarts	WATER
	2 tsp.	SALT for one hour.
Add	½ lb.	WHOLE ONIONS, peeled
	½ lb.	CARROTS, peeled and cut in chunks
	½ lb.	CABBAGE, cut in small wedges
	½ lb.	STRING BEANS, trimmed
	3 cloves	GARLIC, chopped finely.
Simmer	for 1 hour until vegetables are thoroughly cooked.	
Remove	lamb bones and put the mixture through a sieve or food mill.	
Add	4 Tbs.	PEANUT BUTTER thinned with
	1	LEMON (juice of)
	½ cup	COOKED RICE (optional).
Correct the Seasoning	with salt, pepper, etc.	
Serve	in soup bowls, about 1 cup per portion.	

MASCHI | Stuffed Tomato with Chopped Beef

Maschi is also made with cucumbers. The cucumbers are peeled, cut lengthwise, scooped out, filled and finished as below. You may also use eggplants. Peel small eggplants, remove the tops, scoop out interiors and proceed in the same manner. The cucumber dish is garnished with fresh cucumber slices and the eggplant with tomato and cucumber slices overlapping all around the edge.

Yield: 8 portions

In a 9-inch skillet:

Sauté
2 lbs.   CHOPPED BEEF
1 tsp.   SALT
½ tsp.   PEPPER
1 tsp.   GARLIC POWDER (or 2 cloves mashed)
4 Tbs.   CHOPPED FRESH DILL (or 1 tsp. dried dill) in
2 Tbs.   SALAD OIL until meat browns.

Add
1 cup   COOKED RICE and blend.

Cut a Slit in
8 large   TOMATOES (very firm), halfway across the center.

Squeeze
at the sides to open the slit.

Scoop Out
all the flesh from inside of tomatoes with a spoon.

Refill
tomato with beef mixture and close the tomato.

Melt
2 Tbs.   BUTTER and
2 Tbs.   OIL in a large skillet.

Sauté
the tomatoes carefully in the fat, rolling them gently until they become dark red on all sides.

Remove
the tomatoes with the oil and place in a casserole or heavy saucepan.

Prepare
sauce as follows and pour over the tomatoes:

Combine
2 6-oz. cans   TOMATO PASTE thinned with
2 6-oz. cans   WATER
½ tsp.   SALT
1 tsp.   CINNAMON
1 tsp.   GARLIC POWDER.

Simmer
the tomatoes gently over low flame for 10 to 15 minutes until sauce is cooked.

Remove
carefully to a 15-inch round platter.

Surround
with raw   TOMATOES cut in thick slices.

Top Each Slice
with   GREEN OLIVES

If there is more *Maschi* filling left over after filling the tomatoes place it in a suitable pan and bake it alongside the tomatoes.

SALATA MA JIBNA | Salad with Parmesan Cheese

Yield: 8 small salads

In a 2-quart salad bowl:

Combine	1 cup	ONIONS, cut in slivers or thin slices
	1 cup	CABBAGE, cut in slivers or thin slices
	½ cup	CARROTS, cut in very thin rounds (slices)
	1 cup	TOMATOES, cut in ½-inch dice.
Toss with	¼ cup	OLIVE OIL
	¼ cup	LEMON JUICE
	2 Tbs.	VINEGAR (white)
	1 tsp.	SALT
	¼ tsp.	COARSE BLACK PEPPER.
Sprinkle	1 clove	GARLIC (mashed)
	¼ cup	GRATED CHEESE (Oriental or Parmesan) over salad.
Serve	in small individual salad dishes.	

SHATA | Hot Spice Accompaniment

Yield: 8 portions

In a 1-quart salad bowl:

Combine	1 cup	LEMON JUICE
	3 cloves	GARLIC, mashed.
Blend in	3 Tbs.	CRUSHED RED PEPPER
	1 tsp.	BLACK PEPPER
	1 tsp.	SALT.
Place	in small ramekin dishes and serve with entrées.	

CREME CARAMELA | Sudanese Caramel Custard

Yield: 1-quart mold

In a 2-quart bowl:

Beat | 8 | EGGS with
| 1 quart | MILK and
| ½ cup | SUGAR until mixture is frothy.

Add | 1 oz. | BUTTER, melted and
| 1 Tbs. | VANILLA (or banana extract if available).

In a 1½-quart (6-cup) star-shaped aluminum cake pan:

Melt | ½ cup | SUGAR and burn to caramel stage.

Rotate the pan to spread caramel all around the sides.

Beat the egg mixture again.

Pour it quickly into the cake pan.

Cover the pan with aluminum foil which has been well buttered on the under side.

Place the pan in a larger pan half filled with water (as you would do a custard).

Bake at 350° for 30 minutes.

Remove cover and test with a silver knife (when it comes out clean, custard is done).

Chill until thoroughly cold.

Turn the CARAMELA out onto a 10- to 12-inch platter.

Garnish with MARASCHINO or CANDIED CHERRIES on top and sides.

CINNAMON TEA

Prepare English tea according to package directions (use loose tea). Tea should be infused until it is a bright orange color. Upon serving, place ½-inch pieces of stick cinnamon in small tea cups and pour hot tea over the cinnamon. Serve with lump sugar.

When a Fish Pyramid with Green Sauce was served to us we thought the dish was such a great idea, we decided to suggest it as an additional dish you may want to serve at your Sudanese dinner. It is very easy to make. It can be served as a salad in place of the *Salata*.

FISH PYRAMID WITH GREEN SAUCE

Yield: 8 portions

Combine	2 lbs.	COOKED FISH, boned and flaked (use haddock, halibut or any white fish)
	1 cup	CORE of the CABBAGE, sliced very thin.
	2	TOMATOES, cut in small cubes.
	½ tsp.	BLACK PEPPER
	1 tsp.	SALT
	2 Tbs.	LEMON JUICE
	¼ cup	MAYONNAISE or enough to just hold mixture together.
Shape		into a pyramid on a 12-inch plate (with hands moistened with water).
Combine	½ cup	MAYONNAISE
	¼ cup	LEMON JUICE
	½ tsp.	SALT
	¼ tsp.	BLACK PEPPER
	½ cup	FRESH CHOPPED DILL or 1 Tbs. dried dill. If dried dill is used add ¼ cup chopped parsley to give the sauce its characteristic green color.
	¼ cup	PICKLE RELISH.
Pour		the Green Sauce over the pyramid.
Garnish		around edge of plate with
	2	HARD-BOILED EGGS sliced and
	2	TOMATOES cut in slices, alternately overlapping each other around the plate
	¼ cup	BLACK OLIVES uniformly placed around the edge of the plate with
	4 or 5	PARSLEY SPRIGS.

Morocco

The cuisine of Morocco is rated among the best in the world, and rightly so. There are few places where food is more carefully and artistically prepared, more delightfully served, and more enjoyed than in this country.

Cooking in Morocco falls into two specific categories. The first, intended for important guests, is the work of skilled chefs. It requires such intensive supervision that the host does not participate. He merely oversees the banquet with his sons and servants. No women are present. The men squat on mattresses or pillows around low, beautifully inlaid tables. A silver ewer of perfumed water is taken around and poured over three fingers of the right hand of each guest.

The host claps his hands and the meal begins. One course after another—each delicacy is served until *Chban*—complete satiation—is achieved. Again the silver ewer filled with warm water is presented to clean the mouth, lips, and hands. The meal is a feast for the gods and indeed it begins and ends with *Bsmillah*—God's blessing.

In the second category of cookery are the wonderful dishes prepared with loving care by the mistresses—*Dadas*—of the homes. Here, where time does not seem to count, she spends hours with her glazed earthenware and copper cooking dishes and her *kanoun,* the movable clay brazier. Her kitchen is austere, and the charcoal which perfumes the kebabs and allows the sauces to simmer is the only source of heat. There are no chairs. A folded carpet serves as a seat. The *Dada* is dressed in a long colorful robe tucked up in front and her wide sleeves are held in place with a twisted cord.

The scents of coriander, cumin, saffron, marjoram, and onion mingle with the pungency of olive oil and the sweetness of sandalwood, mint, and roses, delighting the senses.

How a Dinner Is Served in Morocco

A hostess in Morocco might take a week to prepare a suitable dinner for her honored guests. The meal often consists of as many as fifty courses. It would take a full day just to make *Bstilla*—a crisp pastry, rolled as thin as tissue paper, filled with chicken in a mixture "sweet and peppery, soft and violent."

The dinner starts with *Bstilla,* followed by the typical brochette or kebab flavored with bits of beef or lamb fat. Next comes the *Tajine,* chicken or meat in a spicy stew which has been simmered for many hours, and it is served with a flat bread called *Khubz.*

In Morocco, as in most Arab lands, every household makes its own bread. It is made from semolina flour without shortening or milk. An invocation to God is made before commencing the sacred act of kneading. When the bread has been properly shaped, each family puts its own mark or stamp on it before sending it via the children to a common bakery oven.

After the *Tajine,* a *Batinjaan*—eggplant salad or chopped tomato salad—is served as a separate course. Then comes Couscous, that marvelous Moroccan national dish made of semolina, cooked to perfection, each grain separate from the other. The dinner is completed with slices or wedges of peeled melon, pastries made with honey and almond like the Middle Eastern *Baklava,* and finally a small glass of mint tea.

The dinner following is a very much simplified version, but it is delicious and will give you the "feel" of Morocco. Once you have made the Couscous, it may very well become one of your favorite dishes. This is a delightful dinner to prepare and serve.

How You Can Present a Moroccan Dinner

If feasible, use a low table with cushions on the floor. (Be sure to advise your guests to dress comfortably.) Cover the low table with a bright brocaded cloth and provide your guests with thick towels to cover their knees. You might want to place floral bouquets around the room, but do not have a centerpiece on the table.

Before serving the dinner, walk around the table with an attractive pitcher (silver if possible) filled with warm water which has been scented with cologne or a few drops of perfume. Carry a Turkish towel over your left arm and a small basin in your left hand. Pour a little water over the fingers of each guest, catching the water in the small basin.

Serve tiny kebabs first (with or without a fork) on small plates. As soon as the kebabs have been eaten, remove the plates. The salad may be served as a separate course or may accompany the Couscous. If you serve it separately place the salad (with a fork) in front of each guest. In Morocco, the Couscous is served in a large platter and each guest eats directly from it with a large spoon or he may roll the Couscous up in little balls and pop them into his mouth, but don't expect your guests to do this. You may prefer to place extra plates in front of your guests and ask them to serve themselves.

Slices of melon, watermelon, or canteloupe speared with toothpicks (no plates) are served in a platter right after the Couscous. You might also serve the mint tea at this time, or wait until later to serve it with the honey pastries.

Again the hostess pours water over the fingers of her guests. This is a mark of graciousness and hospitality. At the end of the meal, after tea has been served, bring in a tiny incense burner and light it on the table.

Menu from Morocco

KEBAB KOUTBANE
Tiny Beef Kebabs in a Moorish Marinade

COUSCOUS MARRAKESH
Semolina Grain with Lamb and Chicken

BATINJAAN ZALUD
Salad Made with Eggplant

MELON À LA MOROCAINE

HONEY PASTRIES

MOROCCAN MINT TEA

Shopping List for Eight

Meat and Poultry
1 lb. filet mignon or
  beef steak
½ lb. beef fat (suet)
2½ lbs. boneless lamb
1 3-lb. chicken

Groceries
½ pint olive oil
½ pint peanut oil
1 small can black
  olives
2-oz. jar dried mint
  leaves
1 box loose tea
1 lb. sugar
1 # 2½ can chick peas
  (or ceci beans)
1 pkg. black raisins

Fruits and Vegetables
2 lbs. onions
1 bunch carrots
2 large green peppers
1 lb. yellow squash
1 pkg. frozen string
  beans or peas
2 large eggplants
2 lbs. tomatoes
2 seasonal melons or
  1 watermelon
1 bunch parsley
2 lemons

Special Purchases
In a Middle Eastern or
  gourmet shop:
1 lb. couscous
all condiments and
  spices
honey pastries such as
  Baklava
Incense
In a Japanese or hard-
  ware store:
6-inch bamboo or
  metal skewers
Optional—*cous-
cousière*, available
House of Yemen (see
page 232).

KEBAB KOUTBANE | Appetizer Kebabs in a Moorish Marinade

This typically Moroccan dish is an excellent hors d'oeuvre to serve at any time. It is amazing how the small cubes of suet improve the flavor of the kebab after some of the fat has burned off. The use of suet is particularly effective when cooking kebabs over a charcoal fire and may be successfully substituted in recipes calling for bacon.

Yield: 8 6-inch kebabs

Cut	1 lb.	FILLET OF BEEF OR STEAK into ¾-inch cubes (approximately 32 cubes).
Cut	½ lb.	BEEF SUET into ½-inch cubes.

In an 8 × 10-inch shallow baking dish, prepare the Moorish Marinade:

Combine	¼ cup	ONION, finely chopped and
	2 Tbs.	PARSLEY, finely chopped.
Blend	½ cup	OLIVE or SALAD OIL
	1 tsp.	SALT
	¼ tsp.	PEPPER
	¼ tsp.	GARLIC POWDER
	1 tsp.	GROUND CORIANDER (optional)
	½ tsp.	GROUND CUMIN (optional).

Blend the beef and suet cubes with the marinade and allow the mixture to marinate for several hours.

Thread four pieces of beef alternately with three pieces of suet (start and end with beef) on a 6-inch metal or bamboo skewer.

Grill or **Broil** using a hot fire, basting occasionally with the marinade.

Arrange 1   KEBAB KOUTBANE on a small plate.

Garnish with   TOMATO SLICES and
PARSLEY SPRIGS at the side of the plate.

COUSCOUS MARRAKESH

A *couscousière* is a large double boiler with holes in the bottom of the upper pot allowing its contents to steam. A *couscousière* may be improvised by lining a metal colander with cheese cloth and placing the colander in a 6- or 8-quart pot so that the handles rest on the rim. A piece of heavy-duty foil can serve as a lid.

Yield: 8 portions

Moisten	1 lb.	COUSCOUS in a 3-quart bowl with
	1 cup	COLD WATER to which
	1 Tbs.	SALT has been added.

Stir up with a fork and allow to stand 10 minutes to swell.

Spread the Couscous out in a colander lined with cheese cloth (or in the top of a *couscousière*).

Place the colander over a pan which fits it and is half filled with water.

Cover with aluminum foil and allow to steam for 10 minutes.

In a 6-quart kettle (or bottom of *couscousière*):

Sauté	1 cup	ONIONS coarsely chopped with
	1 tsp.	CORIANDER (powdered)
	1 Tbs.	SALT
	1 tsp.	CRUSHED RED PEPPER
	½ tsp.	SAFFRON
	1 tsp.	POWDERED CUMIN SEED in
	¼ cup	PEANUT OIL until soft but not brown.
Add	2½ lbs.	BONELESS LAMB cut in 2-inch chunks and
	2 quarts	WATER.

Fit the colander (or top of *couscousière*) with the Couscous over the meat, cover it with foil, and allow mixture to simmer gently for 30 minutes.

Add 1 3-lb. CHICKEN cut into 8 pieces *to the stew* and continue cooking for 30 minutes longer.

Stir the Couscous from time to time to make sure the grains are separated.

Add to Stew	1 lb.	CARROTS, scraped and cut in 1-inch chunks
	2	GREEN PEPPERS, cut in ½-inch strips

1 lb.	FRESH TOMATOES, cut in 1-inch wedges
1 lb.	YELLOW SQUASH, peeled and cut in 2-inch slices
12 oz.	FROZEN STRING BEANS (regular cut) or PEAS
1 #2½ can	CHICK PEAS, drained
½ lb.	BLACK RAISINS.

Correct the Seasoning with salt and pepper.

Cook for about 15 minutes or until vegetables are soft but still slightly crisp.

Pour the Couscous into a large (15- to 18-inch) round serving platter.

Make a large hole in the center, pushing the Couscous to the edge of platter.

Arrange meat and vegetables attractively in center, pouring the sauce over all.

Garnish with PARSLEY SPRIGS.

BATINJAAN ZALUD | Eggplant Salad

This Eggplant Salad may also be served as an appetizer. It is an excellent accompaniment to a Couscous, as it is to any of the great entrées of Morocco. Be sure that the salad is very cold when served.

Yield: 8 small salads

Peel 1 or 2 large   EGGPLANTS (approx. 2 lbs.).

Cut into 1-inch slices.

In a 10-inch skillet:

Fry in ½ cup   OLIVE or SALAD OIL until soft.

Mash the eggplant.

Add

¼ cup	ONION finely chopped
3 cloves	GARLIC finely chopped (or 1 tsp. garlic powder)
4 Tbs.	LEMON JUICE
1 tsp.	SALT
¼ tsp.	GROUND PEPPER
1 Tbs.	SUGAR, and blend thoroughly.

Chill in refrigerator.

Heap	½ cup	EGGPLANT MIXTURE on a 6- to 7-inch plate.
Mash		it down to form a circle within 1 inch of edge of plate.
Dribble	with ½ tsp.	OLIVE OIL (if mixture appears dry).
Place	1 slice	TOMATO in center of circle and
	1	BLACK OLIVE in center of tomato.
Garnish with		PARSLEY SPRIGS.

MINT TEA

Yield: 8 servings

	Into a 6-cup glass or china teapot:
Pour	boiling water, rinse and throw the water away.
Put in	3 heaping Tbs. OOLONG TEA (do not use teabags)
	2 heaping Tbs. DRIED MINT LEAVES
	½ cup SUGAR.
Fill	the teapot to the brim with BOILING WATER.
Allow	to steep covered for 5 minutes.
Stir	up the infusion and taste the liquid to see if it is sweet enough.
Strain	into juice glasses (5 to 6 oz.).

Note: Prepare second infusion while the guests are enjoying the first. Add 1 tsp. tea, 1 tsp. mint and 2 Tbs. sugar to the pot. Add boiling water to allow to steep for 5 minutes. Stir again. Taste for sweetness. Strain to serve.

MOROCCAN COCONUT CAKES

You may want to make Moroccan Coconut Cakes, a delicious sweetmeat much like coconut fudge. They are easy to make and ideal to serve later in the evening after the Moroccan dinner.

Yield: 1½ lbs. coconut fudge

In a 2-quart saucepan:

Combine	2 cups	GRATED COCONUT (moist, canned or fresh)
	¾ cup	EVAPORATED MILK
	2 cups	SUGAR
Simmer	gently to 238° or until a soft ball is formed in cold water.	
Add	1 oz.	BUTTER and
	2 Tbs.	LEMON RIND.
Cool	to room temperature in the pan.	
Beat	as you would fudge until thick and glossy.	
Pour	into a square (8 x 8-inch) pan lined with wax paper.	
Chill	and cut into 1-inch squares.	

HONEY PASTRIES

Purchase	small honey pastries in any Middle Eastern food shop. Ask for Baklava. In Morocco it is called *Kab El Ghzal*.
Allow	one or two pastries per guest.
Place	them on a platter lined with a paper doily.
Serve	them on dessert plates with forks.

MELON A LA MOROCAINE

Use	any melon in season or watermelon but be certain that it is very ripe.
Cut	the melon into ½-inch slices and remove the rind.
Cut	again into 3-inch pieces and arrange them attractively on a platter.
Garnish	the platter with sprigs of fresh mint or parsley.
Spear	the melon pieces with colored toothpicks.
Pass	the platter to your guests. No dishes are used with this course.

PEASANT PANCAKES

Here's another outstanding sweet of Morocco which you might want to serve instead of the honey pastries.

Yield: 8 servings

In a 1-pint bowl:

Cut 4   BANANAS (peeled) in ½-inch slices.

Add ½ cup   APRICOT LIQUEUR and marinate for ½ hour.

In a 1-quart bowl:

Place 1 cup   PANCAKE MIX following package directions to make a thick pancake batter using the above liqueur drained from the bananas as part of the liquid.

Add bananas to the batter and stir thoroughly.

In a 9-inch skillet:

Heat ¼ inch   COOKING OIL.

Drop the mixture by tablespoonfuls (2 or 3 pieces of banana in each spoon) into the hot fat until golden brown on both sides.

In a 1-pint bowl:

Combine
½ cup   SOFT BREAD CRUMBS made by grating fresh bread
3 Tbs.   MELTED BUTTER
4 Tbs.   SUGAR
1 tsp.   GROUND GINGER.

Place   3 or 4   PEASANT PANCAKES on dessert plates.

Sprinkle   1 to 2 Tbs.   CRUMB MIXTURE over the pancakes.

Note: Crystallized ginger may be used instead of ground ginger, in which case use 2 Tbs. sugar and 2 Tbs. crystallized ginger, minced finely.

Senegal

Senegal is a semitropical country; warm, sunny and colorful. Nowhere in Africa do the women wear more exquisite fabrics—the brilliant swatches of cloth wound around them and arranged on their heads in enormous bandanas. They have the elegant bearing of women accustomed to carrying bundles or jugs of water on their heads. They like to hold in their mouths tiny twigs made from a special bark and sometimes decorated, with which they rub their teeth from time to time. The men also present an interesting picture in their long, bright, loose "boo-boos" and skullcaps.

The food markets of Senegal teem with color—the bright garb of the vendors blending with their wares of tropical fruits and vegetables. Peanuts are the main crop of Senegal and everywhere the aroma of roasted peanuts permeates the air. Seafood is the mainstay of the diet. The meats eaten less frequently are beef, lamb, and chicken. You'll find no pork, as many Senegalese are Muslims.

The influence of French food in Senegal is unmistakable, yet Senegalese food has a quality of its own, with dishes from many other parts of the world and other parts of Africa incorporated into the cuisine. Rice is the main starch, with the Couscous of northern Africa also being a great favorite.

Dakar, hot and humid but lovely, is the most important city of Senegal. Here one can have fabulous meals at Le Baobab, Tam Tam, and Les Cannibales Deux—restaurants which could compete with the finest anywhere. Gabriel, our handsome, tall (6-foot 4-inch) taxi driver, took us to the outskirts of Dakar where he and his friends have their lunch and we found delicious *Thiou à la Viande*, a meat stew. In the Casamance region north of Dakar, *Yassa,* a chicken specialty with onions and lemon, is prepared. In the village of Soumbedioune, where Senegalese crafts are displayed and where you will see fishermen bringing their catch in from the sea, you may have *Thebouidienne,* the freshly caught fish simmered with vegetables, including white and sweet potatoes, poured over large mounds of white rice.

How a Dinner Is Served in Senegal

When dining in one of the excellent Senegalese restaurants, you will select an appetizer from a list of twenty or twenty-five, all prepared with great care. The soups will be rich and full-bodied. There will be entrées in abundance; *Yassa, Mafe,* and beautiful Couscous among them. Then a long list of fancy desserts, all served with great flair.

Or you might be served at one of the open-air restaurants where food is cooked on small *fournières,* or broilers, which look like hibachis. They average about 15 inches in diameter and are sometimes round and sometimes square. The *fournière* has a grate at the bottom and heat is regulated by adding or removing hot charcoal with tongs as required. (At one school we visited there were about fifty of them in the new home-economics department where cooking classes were about to begin.)

In a Senegalese home you would follow the custom of pouring water over your hands as you enter the dining area and then you would wipe them on a common cloth. After the guests are seated you would probably be served a stew-type dish with rice such as *Thiou au Poulet,* pronounced "chew," a special chicken stew; *Mafe aux Arachid,* meat stew with ground-nuts; or *Thebouidienne,* the delightful fish dish (all included in the recipe section). These would be served in deep enamel bowls, each seeming to be enough for three or four people. Then you would proceed to dip in with the first three fingers of your right hand. This takes getting used to but, once mastered, does seem to add to the food. Fruits would be served as the dessert, followed by coffee and tea.

How You Can Present a Senegalese Dinner

A Senegalese dinner should be served with dignity and elegance. Use brightly colored tablecloths with contrasting napkins for a startling effect. Set your table with scented candles to evoke the perfume of the lush green Casamance region of Senegal where lemons and onions are combined for the Chicken *Yassa.* Have fresh flowers in reds and yellows to suggest the vivid colors of the flower markets. Decorate the table with

African artifacts if you have them. Dishes should be plain white china or glass as a contrast to this color.

If you want to serve a cocktail, try the Senegali Sunshine, which you will find in the beverage section.

Start dinner with the *Avocat aux Crevettes.* Another appetizer you might consider is *Assiette Cannibale* of Senegal (in the recipe section). The *Yassa* is served individually from the kitchen and is followed by *La Salade Côte Cap Verte.* Salads are often eaten after the main course in Senegal.

When presenting the dessert, explain that Mamadou is the young owner of Les Cannibales Deux Restaurant in Dakar who went to Paris to learn French cooking techniques. The Banana Glace is his own creation and his most popular dessert.

Demitasse is served in the living room after dinner. You may want to serve some "Five-Cent Cookies" (see page 45) at this time or later in the evening.

Menu From Senegal

AVOCAT AUX CREVETTES
Avocado Stuffed with Shrimp

YASSA AU POULET DE LA CASAMANCE
Barbecued Chicken in a Rich Onion and
Lemon Sauce over Rice

SALADE CÔTE CAP VERTE
Chopped Egg Salad

MAMADOU'S BANANA GLACE

DEMITASSE

Shopping List for Eight

Poultry, Fish	Vegetables and Fruits	Groceries
4 2½-lb. chickens	2 large or 3 small	1 jar pimientos
1½ lbs. shrimp	avocados	1 quart salad oil
(15 to 20 per lb.)	6 lemons	1 pint tarragon vinegar
Dairy	2 heads lettuce	1 pint bottled lemon
1 dozen eggs	1 lb. tomatoes	juice
1 pint heavy cream	5 lbs. Spanish onions	2 lbs. rice
½ pint yogurt	1 dozen bananas	1 box black raisins
	1 bunch parsley or	1 lb. shelled peanuts
	watercress	1 package slivered
		almonds
		1 jar candied fruit or
		maraschino cherries
		French bread

AVOCAT AUX CREVETTES SÉNÉGALAISES | Avocado Stuffed with Shrimp

This appetizer is really astonishing. It may seem like a lot of work, but it is well worth the effort. The blending of mashed avocado and chick peas combined with shrimp and garnishes makes an intriguing combination of flavors that is unusual and delicious.

Yield: 8 portions

In a 2-quart bowl:

Mash	2 large	AVOCADOS, peeled (or 3 small) with
	4 Tbs.	LEMON JUICE and
	4 Tbs.	PLAIN YOGURT (or sour cream)
Shred	1 head	LETTUCE and place in a 1-quart bowl.

For individual serving:

Place	1 cup	SHREDDED LETTUCE on a salad plate.
Arrange	½ cup	COOKED CHICK PEAS or BLACK-EYED PEAS, seasoned lightly with salt, in center of lettuce.
Cover peas with	3 to 4 Tbs.	AVOCADO MIXTURE (above).
Arrange	2 slices	TOMATO, cut thickly and topped with
	1 Tbs.	CHOPPED SPANISH ONION at one side of avocado.
Place	2 quarters	HARD-BOILED EGG, one each at opposite sides.
Spread	1 slice	PIMIENTO across egg as a garnish.
Arrange	3 large	COOKED SHRIMP in a row on top of avocado.
Garnish with	1 or 2 sprigs	PARSLEY or WATERCRESS.

YASSA AU POULET DE LA CASAMANCE | Barbecued Chickens with Lemon and Onions over Rice

Note that chicken in the *Yassa* is marinated, partially broiled or barbecued to obtain required browning, and then finished in the oven, smothered in the onion-lemon sauce. For the onion lover (and we belong to the Onion Lover's League), this dish is superb.

Yield: 8 portions

Rub	1	LEMON, cut in half heavily over
	4 2½-lb.	CHICKENS cut in halves.
Spread		chickens out in a 12 x 18 x 2-inch baking pan.
Cover with	3 lbs.	WHITE ONIONS, thinly sliced
	½ cup	CHOPPED PARSLEY
	1 Tbs.	COARSE BLACK PEPPER
	1 Tbs.	COARSE SALT
	3	BAY LEAVES
	1 tsp.	THYME
	1 tsp.	CRUSHED RED PEPPER (optional).
Pour	1 cup	LEMON JUICE and
	1 cup	SALAD OIL over the chickens.

Allow to marinate for 30 minutes.

Remove the chickens and *broil* (preferably over charcoal) until chickens brown on all sides and are about half done.

Simmer the onion mixture above over direct heat stirring up from bottom to prevent onions from browning. Onions should remain white. Cook no longer than 5 minutes.

Return chickens to pan, smothering them with the onions.

Pour	1 quart	CHICKEN STOCK (including giblets) over the mixture.

Bake at 375° for 20 minutes until onions turn a light golden color.

Cook	½ to 1 lb.	WHITE RICE as directed on package.
Place	serving of	COOKED RICE on a dinner plate.
Top with	1	BROILED CHICKEN HALF.
Cover with	½ to 1 cup	YASSA ONION MIXTURE.
Garnish with		WATERCRESS or PARSLEY.

LA SALADE CÔTE CAP VERTE | Salad with Chopped Eggs

La Salade is so important in French cuisine that in Senegal it may be used both as an appetizer or as a salad following the main dish. When serving the entrée, present the *Yassa* first and then bring your *Salade Côte Cap Verte.* It is correct to serve French bread at this time.

Yield: 8 salads

In a salad bowl:

Combine 2 to 3 cups any available greens as LETTUCE, SPINACH, WATERCRESS, ROMAINE, cut in coarse chunks.

Arrange in mounds on 6- to 7-inch salad plates.

Chop 4 HARD BOILED EGGS finely (or put through sieve).

Sprinkle eggs heavily over the mound of greens.

In a jar:

Combine 1 cup SALAD OIL (use part olive oil if possible)
1/2 cup TARRAGON VINEGAR
1 tsp. GARLIC POWDER (or crushed cloves)
1 tsp. SALT
1/2 tsp. FRESHLY GROUND PEPPER
1 Tbs. SALAD HERBS
2 Tbs. HONEY.

Shake thoroughly. Serve dressing separately.

MAMADOU'S BANANA GLACE

This double-strength banana dessert beats a banana split halfway to Dakar! Served with an excellent demitasse, it is a delicious and sophisticated dessert.

Yield: 8 portions

In an electric blender (or by hand):

Beat 4 BANANAS to a pulp.

Add 1 pint HEAVY CREAM and
1/2 cup SUGAR.

Beat	until frothy.	
Pour	into freezer trays and freeze for 1 to 2 hours until partially firm.	
Cut	8	BANANAS in half lengthwise and then in half across.
Place	1	BANANA (4 pieces in a row side by side) on a dessert plate.
Spread	the frozen bananas uniformly over the fresh bananas when ready to serve.	
Sprinkle	each serving with	

½ tsp.	CHOPPED CANDIED FRUITS as ANGELICA or RED CHERRIES
1 tsp.	BLACK RAISINS
1 Tbs.	CHOPPED PEANUTS
1 Tbs.	SLIVERED ALMONDS.

DEMITASSE DAKAR

How to make a really good demitasse:

Measure	¼ lb.	DRIP GRIND COFFEE in a 2-quart glass or enamel saucepan.
Stir in	1	EGG, slightly beaten and enough water to mix thoroughly (about ½ cup).
Pour	1 quart	RAPIDLY BOILING WATER over the coffee and stir up.
Bring	slowly to a boil, stirring occasionally.	
Remove	from heat, cover, and allow to stand for 3 to 4 minutes.	
Strain	through fine sieve or cheese cloth into hot serving pot.	
Pour	in small demitasse cups. Serve black.	

PEANUT ICE CREAM

Senegal is the peanut capital of the world. It is therefore fitting to serve peanuts in some form at your Senegalese dinner. You might try peanut ice cream as served at Le Basbab Restaurant in Dakar.

Yield: 1½ quarts

In a 2-quart saucepan:

Immerse 1 14-oz. can EVAPORATED MILK in boiling water to cover and continue boiling for 20 minutes.

Chill the can thoroughly for several hours with a 2-quart bowl and egg beater.

Whip the chilled evaporated milk in the cold bowl with the cold egg beater.

Add 4 Tbs.   LEMON JUICE and
½ cup   SUGAR.

In a 3-quart bowl
Combine 1 cup   PEANUT BUTTER with
1 can   CONDENSED MILK and
¼ cup   MILK

Fold the whipped mixture carefully into the peanut butter mixture, until smooth.

Pour into freezer trays or into a 6-cup mold and freeze.

THE FIVE-CENT COOKIE

To carry through the Senegalese atmosphere, make a simplified version of the *Cinq Centimes* (the Five-Cent Cookie) you find in the market places of Dakar. Serve them later in the evening after your Senegalese dinner.

Purchase 3-inch sugar cookies at the grocery or bakery.

Spread each with peanut butter within a half inch of the edge.

Sprinkle each with coarsely chopped peanuts.

Arrange attractively on doily-lined platters and pass them to your guests. The youngsters will also adore these cookies.

There are more recipes from Senegal in the recipe section. Do try *Mafe aux Légumes Arachid* (beef stew made with peanut butter) and *Thebouidienne.*

Kenya

Kenya is perhaps the best-known country in Africa to Europeans and Americans through literature, such as the books of Robert Ruark, and through films. Nairobi has long been the center for those setting out on safari—not only hunters but wild-life lovers who take cameras in lieu of guns. Many facilities are available for this sport, such as Tree Tops where one can spend the night watching the bush animals as they make their way to salt licks and watering places.

Our safari, of course, was for recipes and menus, and we were frequently told that we had come to the wrong place. "You couldn't have come to Kenya for the food!" was a common reaction.

We found to our dismay that there were no restaurants serving dishes native to Kenya. Nor were there cookbooks to which we could refer. We finally found one cookbook called *Kenya Kitchen*, but in the main the recipes were of English and American dishes. We did find one recipe, which we have included here, for *Samosas*, the little three-cornered pastries filled with meats.

We discovered that the really delicious cooking of Kenya is being done by the Kikuyu, the Abaluhya, and the Luo tribes. We visited with them and were delighted with their wonderful dishes. The most important dish of the Kikuyu is *Irio*, a seasoned puree of peas, corn, and potatoes. The *M'chuzi wa kuku* and the *M'baazi* are wonderful dishes. *Kariokor* is a delicious way to barbecue meat.

How a Dinner Is Served in Kenya

Two separate menus represent the foods of the Kenyan African. In one, *Irio* is the mainstay, and in the other it is *Ugali.*

The hostess opens the door dressed in a bright floor-length skirt and a striking bandanna wound loosely about her head. She stands there, hands outstretched, to bid you welcome. It is a touching gesture of hospitality. It is early for luncheon, so she brings in a pot of rather weak tea which she serves in small cups with tiny bananas to take the edge off your hunger. Amazingly, it does not spoil your appetite, as one might suppose, and just about holds you until luncheon is ready.

Our hostess returns to the kitchen to pound the groundnuts (peanuts) for the Groundnut Soup. She brings the thick wooden pestle down into the wooden bowl rhythmically until the peanuts are thoroughly pulverized. (Lucky are we who merely open a jar of peanut butter.) She makes the soup by adding 2 cups of water to 2 cups of groundnuts (use peanut butter) and ½ tsp. salt, and simmers it until it becomes very thick. She then thins it back to a soup consistency with milk. She serves this excellent soup in little bowls.

After the soup, all the remaining dishes are placed on the table at one time, each in a decorated calabash (African bowl).

In the homes of the Abaluhya the important course is *Ugali.* For breakfast, the same cornmeal cooked to a thin gruel-like consistency is called *Uji.* There is a light *Ugali* made from cornmeal and a dark *Ugali* made from millet flour. Also served are dishes like *M'baazi* (pea beans), which is sometimes an appetizer as well as a main dish, *M'chuzi Wa Kuku* (chicken in coconut) or *Samaki Na Nazi* (fish and coconut). A stunning dish is *Ndizi,* bananas cooked in banana leaves see page 189).

In the home of the Kikuyu—the mainstay is *Irio* (see page 52), followed by dishes like *Giteke,* bananas and yams, *Karanga,* beef and potato stew, *Mataha,* beans and corn.

Dessert is generally not served, but fruit like papaya—golden orange, juicy, and succulent—is available. The after-dinner beverage is *Maziwa Ya Kuganda* or sour skimmed milk!

How You Can Present a Kenyan Dinner

There are two suggested menus from which you may choose. In either case, use a bright striped or flowered tablecloth with matching napkins, and tropical decor with flowers and leaves strewn on the table, and some carved artifacts, to suggest the safari and the bush, if you have them. Try to buy calabashes for use as bowls (they can be used in serving most of the African dinners).

The first is the dinner featuring *Irio* (which follows). This should be a sit-down dinner. Each course is dished out in the kitchen and served directly to each person. The Oysters Mombasa, should be presented piping hot on dinner plates, or if you can get rock salt (you'll need about 2 lbs.), heat it in a metal dish in the oven and make a bed of the hot rock salt in large soup plates, setting the oysters on top. These plates will require underliners.

Steak and *Irio*—the green mounds filled with steak fingers in sauce—makes a dramatic entrée. Sauce dishes of salad relish, and *Pilli-pilli* (page 128) accompany the *Irio*.

The dessert, Coupe Mt. Kenya in wine glasses, plus tea or coffee served in the usual manner, makes this a dinner people will talk about for a long time.

The second is the Abaluhya menu, which should be a buffet. All the food is served in calabash bowls placed on the exciting tablecloth decorated with leaves and artifacts. Use Mrs. Habwe's menu on page 55. Each dish is a gem. If you decide to serve *Maziwa Ya Kuganda,* purchase skimmed milk and let it stand out of the refrigerator overnight. Once it has soured, chill it. Be sure it is cold when served. It will not clabber, as it would if there were cream in it. Try it. You may like it more than you think. However, have tea or coffee available as well.

Menu from Kenya

OYSTERS MOMBASA
Baked with a Wine Garlic Butter

STEAK AND IRIO
Kenyan Beef in a Mound of Blended Potatoes

SALAD RELISH

CHAPATIS
Bread of East Africa

COUPE MOUNT KENYA
Diced Pineapple Marinated in Rum
on Mango Ice Cream with Pistachios

Kenyan Tea   Kilimanjaro Coffee

Shopping List for Eight

Meat, fish, etc.
3 lbs. filet mignon or
   lean steak
3 dozen oysters
   (smallest available)

Dairy
1 lb. butter
½ pint heavy cream
1 lb. margarine

Beverages
1 bottle Chablis
1 bottle white rum

Fruits and Vegetables
1 bunch parsley
6 lemons
2 oz. fresh garlic
1 small cabbage
1 lb. Bermuda onions
½ lb. green pepper
1 bunch carrots
4 or 5 mangos
1 fresh pineapple

Groceries
1 16-oz. can peas
1 16-oz. can kernel corn
1 package instant
   potatoes (large)
1 package onion-soup
   mix
1 can condensed milk
1 16-oz. can pineapple
   juice
1 packet pistachio nuts

OYSTERS MOMBASA | Baked with a Wine Garlic Sauce

> Nowhere are oysters more delicious than on the east coast of Africa (except for the tiny Olympia oysters you get at Fisherman's Wharf in San Francisco or in New Orleans).
>
> In Kenya, the oysters are opened and each one goes on its own tiny china ramekin or tiny container which looks like a miniature coaster. Twelve of these little dishes are placed on a large platter with a bowl of dark, dark-red cocktail sauce and slices of lemon. Mombasa, that lovely city on the coast of Kenya, boasts the very best of these small oysters.

Yield: 8 portions (4 oysters per person)

Open 32 SMALL OYSTERS (Bluepoints or Olympias if possible).

Leave them on the half shell and place on baking sheets.

Wine Garlic Sauce

Combine
½ cup	MELTED BUTTER
4 cloves	GARLIC very finely minced
1 cup	CHABLIS
4 Tbs.	CHOPPED PARSLEY
1 tsp.	SALT
1 tsp.	FRESHLY GROUND PEPPER
few drops	TABASCO.

Ladle half of above sauce (1 tsp. per oyster) on each one.

Bake at 350°F. for 6 to 8 minutes.

Ladle the remaining sauce uniformly over the oysters again.

Serve immediately, four per person, with LEMON WEDGES on a 9-inch plate (or on hot rock salt if available).

NYAMA NA IRIO | Steak and Irio

Yield: 8 portions

The Irio:

Drain 1 16-oz. can PEAS and measure the liquid.

Put the peas through a vegetable mill or sieve to make a purée.

Drain 1 16-oz. can KERNEL CORN and add the liquid to that of the peas.

In a 2-quart saucepan:

Prepare 4 cups INSTANT MASHED POTATOES following package directions and using the vegetable liquors as part of the required liquid.

Add 3 Tbs. BUTTER
1 tsp. SALT
¼ tsp. PEPPER.

Blend the purée of peas into the mashed potatoes until a smooth green color results.

Fold in the drained kernel corn.

The consistency should be that of firm mashed potatoes.

The Steak:

In a large skillet:

Cut 3 lbs. FILET MIGNON (or any steak) in a 2 × ½ × ½-inch strips.

Sauté in 4 oz. MARGARINE OR OIL, until lightly browned.

Remove the steak from the skillet.

Blend in 6 Tbs. FLOUR to make a roux.

Add 2 cups ONION SOUP made from a packaged mix and cook to medium-sauce consistency.

Correct the Seasoning with salt, pepper, and a little Tabasco.

Return the steak to the sauce.

Make a large mound (about 1 cup) of *Irio* in center of dinner plate.

Form a hole in the center about 2 inches in diameter.

Fill the hole with ½ cup of the sautéed steak and gravy.

Smooth around edges of the *Irio* so it looks like a volcano.

SALADI | East African Salad Relish

> This salad relish is added to and mixed with the hot spicy food by the guest a little at a time to "cool" the spiciness of the dish and change its texture. If the hostess feels that her dinner is not "hot" enough, a small hot chili pepper is added to the relish.
>
> She may also serve individually or in a bowl additional *pilli-pilli* or hot red pepper dissolved in lemon or tomato sauce.
>
> See page 128 for *Pilli-pilli* Sauce and its variations.
>
> For your Kenyan dinner you might have a cruet of a white French dressing on the table for those who might want to add it to their salad.

Yield: Relish for 8 salads

In a 1-quart bowl:

Combine 2 cups   CABBAGE, finely shredded
         ½ cup   CARROTS in very, very thin slices
         ½ cup   SWEET ONIONS (Bermuda or Spanish or scallions)
         ¼ cup   GREEN PEPPER in fine strips.

Fluff the mixture up.

That's it. There is no dressing or seasoning.

Fill small sauce dishes, allowing about ⅓ cup per person.

COUPE MOUNT KENYA

Any fruit ice cream will serve for the Coupe Mount Kenya, especially peach ice cream. Fruit sherbet may also be used. Canned pineapple may be substituted for the fresh, but it does not have the same zing.

Yield: 1 quart ice cream

Mango Ice Cream

Mash	4 or 5	RIPE MANGOS, peeled and pitted. There should be 2 cups.
Whip	1 cup	HEAVY CREAM with
	½ cup	SUGAR until stiff.

In a 2-quart bowl:

Combine	2 cups	MASHED MANGOS
	2 Tbs.	LEMON PEEL cut in tiny ribbons
	½ cup	CONDENSED MILK
	½ tsp.	SALT.
Fold	in the whipped cream.	
Pour	into freezer trays or a 6-cup mold and freeze.	

Pineapple Rum Sauce

Yield: 1 quart sauce mixture

In a 1-quart sauce pan:

Simmer	1 cup	PINEAPPLE JUICE (canned) and
	1 cup	SUGAR until it dissolves and a syrup is formed.
Add	½ cup	WHITE RUM. Cool.

In a 2-quart bowl:

Cut	3 cups	FRESH PINEAPPLE in ½-inch dice.
Pour	the Pineapple Rum Sauce over the pineapple.	
Marinate	for several hours.	

Place	1 scoop	MANGO ICE CREAM in a 6-oz. wine glass.
Top with	3 to 4 oz.	PINEAPPLE RUM MIXTURE
Garnish with	1 Tbs.	PISTACHIO NUTS, coarsely chopped.

The following Abaluhuya luncheon was our treat at the home of Mrs. Ruth Habwe in Nairobi. Each dish was so outstanding that all the recipes are included in this book. You will find them in the recipe section. In Swahili it reads:

M'BAAZI
Beans in the
Manner of Kenya

N'DIZI
Bananas Steamed in
Banana Leaves

SUMAKI NA NAZI
Fresh Fish in Pink
Coconut Cream

M'CHICHA
Spinach and
Groundnuts

PAPAYA

MAZIWA YA KUGANDA
Sour Skimmed Milk

Tanzania

Tanzania, formerly called Tanganyika, on the east coast of Africa, is known for its tropical beaches, great lakes, huge game areas, and majestic snow-capped Kilimanjaro.

Food throughout much of East Africa is similar and, at first, we found the food to be much like that in Kenya. Yet there are subtle differences. Whenever a dish has a Swahili name, it invariably contains coconut and/or bananas. There is coconut milk and curry (made with home-grown curry differing from the Madras types of curry in its flavor and bright orange color), coconut milk in soups, vegetables, egg dishes, fish, meat and poultry, as well as in dessert dishes. The bananas are used in meat stews as well as with fish and poultry. *Ugali,* the perennial cornmeal porridge, is the major staple. Rice is also frequently eaten.

A visit to the outdoor market of Dar Es Salaam is a rare experience. Under a huge roof vendors sit cross-legged at the sides of their low stands and sell a great variety of fruits and vegetables, chickens, live pigeons, meats, freshly caught fish, and myriad spices. At the "pharmaceutical stands" you can buy many mysterious potions; little bottles to cure you of snake bite, insect bite, or an unwanted lover. There are also brightly colored powders which you can sprinkle on your lover's *Ugali* to make him (or her) more amorous, as well as to heal all manner of other ills.

Little shops abound where you can buy kitchen utensils. We brought back a reed sieve for squeezing coconut, a small seat with a round metal edge upon which one sits to grate the fresh coconut, coconut shell dippers, and a metal brazier.

The people are friendly and hospitable, and a guest is shown great deference. It's hard to leave Dar, and when the time comes you say regretfully, *"Kwa heri ya kuonana."* (Farewell, 'til we meet again.)

How a Dinner Is Served in Tanzania

"Jambo Hodi?" (Hello, may I come in?) you ask in Swahili as you enter a Tanzanian home.

"Karibu" (Draw near, you are welcome) is the reply.

To partake of the Tanzanian repast properly you need to be comfortably dressed, perhaps in slacks and a loose shirt, as you will sit on a mat on the floor in the home of your host.

Your host will dip into the *Ugali* or cassava or rice or other dish with the three fingers of the right hand, and once you have mastered this you will find the taste of the food quite different. You discover how to "work" the stew and vegetables into a loose ball of the right texture so that you can bring it to your mouth without dripping.

The first taste burns your throat slightly, the next taste less so, and you are soon adjusted to the hotness, trying the many dishes spread before you and eating far more than you normally do.

If you are an "honored" guest, as they say in Africa, your hostess has personally selected the duckling which she has cooked with coconut milk. There will also be a banana and meat stew, *Ugali* or rice or potato or perhaps all of these served in huge bowls, and also a vegetable dish like our braised cabbage. Some of these dishes will be cooked with coconut milk and some with groundnuts (peanuts).

Dessert is always fresh fruit of the region. Tanzanian honey is featured at the Kilimanjaro Hotel of Dar Es Salaam, one of the loveliest hotels in Africa. Honey and coconut are fitting accompaniments to Tanzanian fruits and are especially good with pineapple slices. Any fruit drink is called *Squash* throughout Africa. The concentrate may be purchased at the market and is always served at dinner.

Hands are washed before and after the meal and wiped on a towel which is passed around.

The hostess and her family are most gracious. When you leave their home you are accompanied right to the door of your car by the entire family.

"Asante sana" (Many thanks for your hospitality) you say.

How You Can Present a Tanzanian Dinner

Of course you are not expected to serve this dinner on a mat on the floor unless you really want to be authentic.

Set the dining-room table with a plain white cloth as a buffet. A hand of bananas might be the centerpiece, decorated with fresh whole coconuts and interspersed with leaves and flowers. Make it look like Africa. Arrange bridge tables with the necessary number of settings. Napkins should be bright prints.

At the end of the table closest to guests as they come in, stack small soup bowls next to the tureen of coconut bean soup. Ask your guests to serve themselves with soup first and to return for the entrée dishes. Use large soup dishes for the main course.

The Indian *Chapati* bread is eaten in Tanzania as it is over much of East Africa. Recipe is on page 209 should you want to make it.

Have small compote dishes next to the pineapple, and the fruit squash in pitchers on the bridge tables.

Coffee or tea may be served later.

Thin pancakes called *Chapati Majis* are often served as a cake or cookie for dessert with tea or coffee. Make up 4-inch thin pancakes from a pancake mix. Sprinkle with sugar or spread with honey. Fold in half and then in half again. Sprinkle the top with cinnamon sugar.

Menu from Tanzania

COCONUT BEAN SOUP

DUCKLING DAR ES SALAAM

with

BRAISED CABBAGE

and

UGALI
Cornmeal Staple

FRESH PINEAPPLE WITH HONEY

FRUIT SQUASH

Shopping List for Eight

Meat and Poultry	Fruits and Vegetables	Groceries
6-lb. duckling	2 lbs. onions	1 16-oz. can kidney beans (or any dried beans)
	1 lb. green peppers	
	2 lbs. tomatoes	2 pkgs. grated or shredded coconut
	4 bananas (if used with duckling)	½ lb. white rice
	2 lbs. cabbage	1 box farina or grits
	1 large ripe pineapple	1 package bouillon cubes
	1 box strawberries	1 lb. honey
		2 quarts carbonated fruit drink

COCONUT BEAN SOUP

In Tanzania, as in other African countries, soups and sauces are served in a consistency that is as thick as our stews. Coconut Bean Soup would be used there as a meatless main dish by increasing the quantities of beans and rice. However, in adapting this recipe in our test kitchen we thinned it to soup consistency with additional water and served it as a delightful soup course. Any dried beans such as black-eyed peas or pea beans can be used in this soup. Just cover with water and cook until tender before combining them with the other ingredients. Coconut milk and the delicate use of curry give the soup its unusual flavor.

Yield: 2 quarts (8 cups)

		In a 3-quart saucepan:
Sauté	½ cup	ONIONS, chopped finely
	½ cup	GREEN PEPPERS, chopped finely
	1 tsp.	CURRY POWDER
	1 tsp.	SALT
	¼ tsp.	PEPPER in
	3 Tbs.	MARGARINE OR BUTTER until soft but not brown.
Add	1 cup	FRESH TOMATO cut in ½-inch pieces.
Simmer		for two minutes longer.
Add	2½ cups	KIDNEY BEANS (24-oz. can with liquid)
	2 cups	COCONUT MILK (see page 226)
	3 cups	WATER.
Simmer		gently for 10 minutes.
Add	½ cup	COOKED RICE.
Correct the Seasonings		to your taste.
Serve		one-cup portions in attractive soup bowls.
Garnish each bowl with	1 tsp.	SHREDDED COCONUT.

DUCKLING DAR ES SALAAM

Duckling is a great delicacy in Tanzania and is usually served when there are special guests. The same recipe is used for other meats and is particularly good with veal and chicken. Accompaniments are cooked bananas (a must), rice, potatoes, cassava and *Ugali* made with white cornmeal.

Yield: 8 portions

In a 6-quart Dutch oven or baking dish:

Sauté	1 cup	ONIONS finely chopped, and
	1 cup	TOMATOES in small dice, with
	1 tsp.	SALT
	1 tsp.	CURRY POWDER (optional)
	½ tsp.	CRUSHED RED PEPPER (optional) in
	4 Tbs.	OIL or MARGARINE until soft.
Add	1 6-lb.	DUCKLING, cut up into about 12 pieces.
Sauté	the duckling lightly for 2 or 3 minutes.	
Add	2 quarts	WATER
Cover	and simmer for 30 minutes or bake at 350° until duckling is tender.	

Slightly green bananas or plantains may be simmered with the duckling. Or they may be prepared separately and served as a side vegetable. For this allow ½ banana per portion or 4 large bananas.

UGALI | Cornmeal Mush

One of the foods most frequently used in both East and West Africa is a mush or gruel made by pounding fresh corn and squeezing out the cornstarch. When it is cooked in boiling water to a gruel consistency and used as a breakfast cereal it is called *Uji* (*Ogi,* in West Africa). When it is cooked to a thicker consistency, so that it can easily be rolled into a ball, it is called *Ugali* (*Agidi* in West Africa).

As a substitute you can use cornmeal grits or buckwheat grits. Africans in our country use any fine white cereal such as Farina or Cream of Wheat. These cereals are surprisingly tasty when served with meat and poultry gravies. Stone-ground white cornmeal can be purchased in specialty food shops.

For added flavor, try cooking cornmeal grits, farina, or any cereal in chicken or beef stock instead of water. The cereals absorb the flavor of the stock and make an excellent accompaniment for meats. Rice and couscous, that wonderful semolina grain used so abundantly in North Africa, are delicious when prepared in this way.

In Swahili any thick mush is called *Ugali.* There is a light *Ugali* made with cornmeal flour and there is a dark *Ugali* made with millet flour, and often groundnuts (peanuts) are ground in with the mush.

Yield: 8 portions

In a 2-quart saucepan:

Boil rapidly	1 quart	WATER or CHICKEN BROTH.
Add	1 tsp.	SALT and
	1 cup	ANY FINE WHITE CEREAL.

Swirl the cereal into the boiling water and cook according to package directions to a thick heavy mush.

Keep warm over hot water (in a double boiler) until ready to serve.

BRAISED CABBAGE

Yield: 8 portions

In a 3-quart saucepan:

Sauté	½ cup	BERMUDA ONIONS (purple), chopped finely
	1 tsp.	SALT
	¼ tsp.	CRUSHED RED PEPPER in
	2 oz.	OIL or MARGARINE until soft but not brown.
Add	2 lbs.	CABBAGE cut in 1-inch wedges.

Sauté lightly until cabbage begins to lose its crispness.

Add	1 cup	BEEF STOCK (or 1 cup water and 1 bouillon cube).

Correct the Seasoning to your taste.

Simmer for 5 minutes.

Serve in a 2-quart bowl.

SPICY BRAISED CABBAGE

Prepare   the cabbage using the above method, but add the following to the onions: In a small bowl:

Combine   1 tsp.   SALT
½ tsp.   CURRY POWDER
½ tsp.   GARLIC POWDER
¼ tsp.   POWDERED GINGER
½ tsp.   CHILI POWDER.

Sauté   with the onions and proceed as for Braised Cabbage, above.

COCONUT CABBAGE

Use   recipe for Braised Cabbage.

Leave out   the crushed red pepper.

Add   1 cup   COCONUT MILK (see page 226) instead of beef stock.

FRUITS OF AFRICA PIE

Yield: one 9-inch pie

Prepare   one cooked 9-inch pie shell using packaged PIE CRUST.

In a 2-quart saucepan:

Bring   1½ cups   PAPAYA or GUAVA or APRICOT NECTAR to the boiling point.

Dissolve   4 Tbs.   CORNSTARCH in
4 Tbs.   LEMON JUICE.

Add   4 Tbs.   SUGAR and
½ tsp.   SALT.

Add   to the nectar and cook until thick and clear. Cool slightly.

Add   2 cups   DICED FRESH FRUIT such as PAPAYA, PINEAPPLE, MELON, ORANGES, GUAVAS, etc., singly or in combination.

Cool   to room temperature.

Pour   into pie shell. Chill.

Spread with   1 cup   HEAVY CREAM whipped with
4 Tbs.   SUGAR.

Sprinkle   ½ cup   MOIST SHREDDED COCONUT mixed with
½ cup   CHOPPED PEANUTS over the top.

Chill.

Mozambique

The islands of São Tomé and Principe, Cape Verde, and the territories of Portuguese Guinea on the northwest coast of Africa, Angola on the southwest coast, and Mozambique on the southeast are provinces of Portugal. There is great similarity in their foods. Cornmeal, millet, rice, and hot stews, so common in the African diet, are mainstays in all these regions. Our book would be incomplete without some of the outstanding and unusual dishes of Portuguese Africa.

The Portuguese influence is much in evidence, particularly in the use of wine. One such dish is *Matata:* clams cooked in port wine with finely chopped peanuts and tender young greens or fruits. A favorite dish of the interior is *Frango a Cafrial* which means "Chicken, the African way." Chickens heavily rubbed down with *Piri-piri* are roasted over charcoals. They are so peppery that it would be impossible for us to eat them. We have included a modified version of this most interesting dish on page 74. There is also "Chicken, the Portuguese way," made with tomatoes and wine, and we have included this recipe as well.

Caril is the name for curries, also served very "hot" with *Manga Achar,* a special mango chutney that is one of the little dishes accompanying it. The other little dishes contain chopped peanuts, coconut, cucumber, bananas, etc. They are similar to the *Sambals* (relishes) of India.

Fishing is a major industry in both Angola and Portuguese Guinea. The fish of Mozambique and especially the shellfish—lobster tails, shrimp, and prawns—are considered by many to be the most delicious in the world (see page 75 on "How to cook shrimp in the Mozambique manner").

Coffees from Angola, Cape Verde, and São Tomé are among the finest grown anywhere, and tea from the Zambezia region is of outstanding quality. Portuguese wines are an important adjunct to the menu.

How a Dinner Is Served in Mozambique

Mozambique was colonized by Portugal in the fifteenth century, and the Portuguese influence is still very much in evidence. The beautiful seacoast city of Lourenço Marques, the capital of Mozambique, is a miniature Lisbon with its pastel buildings, sidewalk cafés, and tile floors. If you were a house guest in Lourenço Marques, your host would probably invite you to the bullfights on the outskirts of the city—one of the few places in Africa where one can still see this spectacle. On your return, your hostess would spread her dining-room table with an exquisite lace cloth and matching napkins from Madeira or Cape Verde. There would be two wine glasses at each place and flowers in a silver bowl flanked by imposing candelabra would form the centerpiece.

You would then be offered (Scotch) whiskey with soda or water. You may choose (Portuguese) port if you prefer. The dinner then begins with a well-chilled aperitif, either white port or dry Madeira. Red table wine is served with the entrée and with the dessert.

Dinner begins with soup in attractive soup plates. The entrée is then brought to the table in handsome bowls and served by the hostess, accompanied by the wine. *Piri-piri,* the hot pepper relish is passed in a small bowl. Bread is not generally a part of the meal unless it is requested. The salad accompanies the entrée. Lastly fruit macerated in port *vinho* is the *pièce de résistance,* and wine glasses are replenished. The guests then move to the living room where the hostess pours an excellent robust coffee from Angola in demitasse cups or Zambezian tea in larger tea cups. The meal is rounded off with a pony of *Agua Ardente,* a superb Portuguese liqueur.

How You Can Present a Dinner from Mozambique

The presentation of this dinner is unique because the menu and food are from Mozambique but the service and the wines are strictly Portuguese.

If you happen to have a lace tablecloth and napkins, this is an opportunity to put them to use. Decorate the table with attractive candelabra, using white or beige candles, and a low floral centerpiece. Bring out your best china, silverware, and wine glasses.

Although the table is formally set, the dinner itself is quite informal.

Set up a cocktail bar in another room with Scotch, soda, water, and ice and a bottle of port wine. Serve black olives and Portuguese cheeses as hors d'oeuvres.

At the dining-room table, dinner is approached in a leisurely fashion. Pour a well-chilled white port wine (or any white wine) as an aperitif. The soup may be ladled into large soup plates from a tureen at the table or served from the kitchen. *Matata,* the unusual clam-peanut entrée, and white rice in two attractive bowls are served by the hostess or passed. A small bowl of *Piri-piri* is placed on the table. Individual salads are set down at the left of each plate.

Provide knives and forks for the dessert. A glass bowl containing the fruit in wine is set before the hostess, who turns the fruit over in the bowl before arranging it on the dessert dishes. A red port wine may be poured with the dessert.

Coffee in demitasse cups or tea are taken in the living room after dinner with an after-dinner cordial or liqueur (if you cannot get *Agua Ardente*).

After your Mozambique dinner, play recordings of the Fado singers, an important part of Portuguese night life. Dressed in black shawls, they moan the sad songs of mournful women, singing of love and its disappointments.

Menu from Mozambique

SOPA DE FEIJAO VERDE
String Bean Soup

MATATA
Clam and Peanut Stew

ARROZ
Rice

PIRI-PIRI
Hot Pepper

SALADA DE PERA ABACATE
Avocado and Tomato Salad

ANANAS CON VINHO DO PORTO
Pineapple with Ruby Port Wine

ZAMBEZIAN TEA   **PORT WINE**   **ANGOLAN COFFEE**

Shopping List for Eight

Beverages	Fruits and Vegetables	Groceries
dry Madeira	1 head lettuce	4 8-oz. cans chopped clams
Agua Ardente or any after-dinner liqueur	2 lbs. tomatoes	1 pint bottle lemon juice
red port wine	2 avocados	1 16-oz. can peach slices
Portuguese table wine	1 lb. potatoes	1 lb. peanuts (shelled)
	2 lbs. onions	1 lb. white rice
	1 lb. string beans	1 lb. cashew nuts
	1½ lbs. fresh young spinach	¼ lb. tea and/or
	1 fresh pineapple	1 lb. coffee

SOPA DE FEIJAO VERDE | String Bean Soup

Yield: 2 quarts (8 cups)

In a 3-quart saucepan:

Bring to a boil	1½ quarts	WATER.
Add	2 tsp.	SALT
	½ tsp.	PEPPER
	3 large	POTATOES, cut in chunks
	2 medium	TOMATOES, cut in chunks
	2 large	ONIONS, cut in chunks.

Simmer   for 30 minutes or until vegetables are tender.

Purée   through a sieve or food mill. (It should be a thin purée.)

Add   1 lb.   FRESH STRING BEANS, cut across in *thin slices.*

Simmer   for about 10 minutes until beans are tender.

Correct the Seasoning

Serve   in bowls.

It will take a little time to slice the fresh string beans in very thin (straight-across) slices. As an adaptation and for the sake of speed, here's the fast modern version of this lovely soup:

Combine	1 cup	INSTANT POTATOES
	1 Tbs.	ONION POWDER
	1½ quarts	BOILING WATER
	1 6-oz. can	TOMATO SAUCE

No puréeing is necessary.

Cut   1 package   FROZEN ITALIAN BEANS (thawed) in thin slices.

Add   to the mixture above.

Simmer   until beans are done.

Serve   in bowls or large soup plates.

MATATA | Clam and Peanut Stew

Matata is a typical Mozambique entrée made with pumpkin leaves. We have used spinach as a substitute. This is one dish that wasn't influenced by the cooking of Portugal. Imagine a combination like clams and peanuts and tender young greens! You may want to hold out the crushed red pepper. Start without it and add it gradually, with discretion.

Yield: 8 portions

In a 4-quart saucepan

Sauté	1 cup	ONIONS chopped finely in
	2 oz.	OLIVE OIL until soft but not brown.
Add	4 cups	CANNED CHOPPED CLAMS
	1 cup	PEANUTS, chopped finely
	2	TOMATOES cut in small pieces
	1 Tbs.	SALT
	½ tsp.	BLACK PEPPER
	1 tsp.	CRUSHED RED PEPPER.
Simmer		gently for 30 minutes.
Add	1½ lbs.	FRESH SPINACH (young leaves) chopped finely.
Cover tightly		and, as soon as leaves have wilted, *Matata* is ready to serve.
Correct the Seasoning		
Cook	2 cups	WHITE RICE in
	5 cups	BOILING SALTED WATER until tender.
Serve		over rice.

PIRI-PIRI

Combine	4 Tbs.	LEMON JUICE
	4 Tbs.	OLIVE OIL
	4 Tbs.	COARSE RED PEPPER
	1 Tbs.	SALT
	1 tsp.	GARLIC POWDER.
Place		in a small bowl.
Serve		with a tiny spoon. Use sparingly.

SALADA PERA DE ABACATE | Avocado Salad

Canned peach slices may be added to the Avocado Salad—in which case use one slice of tomato and two to three peach slices.

This Lemon Dressing is excellent on a tossed green salad or hearts of lettuce. It is light and easy to make.

Yield: 8 small salads

Cut	1 head	ICEBERG LETTUCE down in ¾-inch round uniform slices.
Arrange		one slice on each salad plate.
Alternate	2	TOMATOES cut in 8-inch uniform slices overlapping with
	2	AVOCADOS cut in thick uniform slices
		across the lettuce in a straight line.
Spoon	2 Tbs.	of the following Lemon Dressing over the avocado salad:

Lemon Dressing

Combine	1 cup	LEMON JUICE (bottled)
and	1 cup	OLIVE OIL
Shake	1 cup	PEACH SYRUP (from a can or use any fruit syrup)
	1 tsp.	SALT
	1 tsp.	SALAD HERBS
	¼ tsp.	PEPPER.
Serve		as a side salad.

FRESH PINEAPPLE IN PORT WINE

Yield: 8 portions

Peel	1 large	RIPE SWEET PINEAPPLE
Cut		in ½ inch slices and remove the core.
Sugar		each slice lightly on both sides.
Place		in a 2-quart glass or china bowl.
Cover		with ½ cup RED PORT WINE.
Allow		to stand for several hours.
Turn		the pineapple in the wine from time to time.

Turn   again just before serving on dessert dishes.

Serve   with spoons and forks.

Cashew nuts are one of the major crops of Mozambique. It would be quite appropriate to sprinkle cashew nuts on the pineapple or to pass a bowl of cashew nuts with the dessert or as a snack later in the evening.

TEA OR COFFEE

Tea plantations are situated in the Zambezia region of Mozambique. That is why your menu reads Zambezian tea and Angolan coffee. If you can purchase this tea or coffee in a gourmet or specialty shop, it would add greatly to your dinner.

If you prefer you could serve either of the following entrées in place of the *Matata*.

FRANGO A CAFRIAL | Barbecued Chicken

In Mozambique about 4 Tbs. of hot red pepper are used in the *Cafrial*. In this recipe, crushed red peppers may be substituted. 1 tsp. cayenne pepper will give quite a "bite," so if you prefer to hold the seasoning and add it after the chickens are cooked, cut down on the amount given.

Yield: 8 half chickens

Combine   1 tsp.   CAYENNE PEPPER
1 Tbs.   SALT
1 tsp.   GARLIC POWDER
½ tsp.   GROUND GINGER
1 tsp.   PAPRIKA and
½ cup   SALAD OIL, and blend thoroughly.

Rub   4 2½-lb.   WHOLE CHICKENS with the seasoned oil on all sides thoroughly.

Roast, Broil, or Barbecue   the chickens in your favorite manner, basting them from time to time with the seasoned oil until chickens are done. Cut chickens in half.

Serve   with plenty of white rice (allow 1 cup cooked rice per person).

SHRIMP AND SEAFOOD THE MOZAMBIQUE WAY

	In a 2-quart saucepan:	
Place	1 lb.	RAW SHRIMP (with or without shells)
	3 cups	WATER warm from the tap
	1 tsp.	SALT
	1 tsp.	CRUSHED RED PEPPER, or use a few drops Tabasco.
Squeeze	3	LEMON WEDGES into the pot and toss the lemon in it.

Bring the shrimp up to the boiling point and turn off the flame. Cover.

Allow to stand for 30 minutes. Shrimp will be thoroughly cooked.

Devein, wash in clear water and chill.

Serve with *Piri-piri* (see page 72).

Note how tender the shrimp become, cooked this way. And don't waste that water. Plan to use it in a chowder or in a sauce. Taste it. It's great! Other seafood may be prepared in this manner.

The Island of Zanzibar

When the wind blows in the right direction, the fragrance of spice is deliciously strong, and you know you are in Zanzibar, the Spice Island, with its cloves and cinnamon, lichee nuts, cocoa beans, and coconut. A tiny island, it is a part of Tanzania, the name deriving from a combination of the names of the two formerly separate states, Tanganika and Zanzibar.

On our visit to the island, the political situation did not permit us to move about freely, but we were able to walk through the narrow streets and visit the marketplace. The food market is just as we had imagined it. Fruits and vegetables are abundant. Barefoot vendors in colorful balloon pants and skull caps sit cross-legged on the ground before neat rows or piles of their produce. Bananas and plantains, cassava, addoes (a potato-like vegetable), hot red peppers, and all kinds of green vegetables are in plentiful supply in their stalls.

We bought little cellophane bags of colored coconut, purple and pink, and surprisingly delicious. We stuffed ourselves with sticky sesame candy and hot baked sweet potatoes, toasted corn, and baked cassava. Three boys passed with baskets made of palm leaves on their heads—one carried papayas, the second bananas, and the third coconuts. We mused on the many delicacies one could make with these three fruits alone.

A drive through the countryside provided many interesting experiences. In a visit to one of the circular huts, we were most impressed by the delightful hospitality of the women so eager for company. Our hostess was cooking a silvery liquid shimmering with small round fish (somewhat like our butterfish) in a luscious lemon-flavored sauce. The aroma of whole sweet potatoes baking on a three-stone hearth filled the air. The amazing coolness of the mud hut made us reluctant to leave, but our guides hustled us off. On our way to the car we did stop to contemplate the profusion of fresh fruits and nuts at arm's reach. We picked grape fruits, lemons, lichee nuts, and long thin reeds of lemon grass, and cut cinnamon bark from the cinnamon tree.

Although we were not able to stay for this repast, it is safe to assume that it would have been served in the same manner as in Tanzania. You have the choice of presenting the menu in the native manner (see Tanzania) or as it was served at the Zanzibar Hotel with waiter service.

We were not permitted to lunch in a native restaurant and were taken instead (to our disappointment!) to the Zanzibar Hotel, where all visitors and tourists are asked to eat. But the luncheon at the hotel exceeded our expectations and was so well served that we decided to include the menu here. It took a bit of doing to get the recipes, but here they are, easy to make and simple to serve.

How You Can Present a Zanzibar Dinner

Make this a formal dinner. The tablecloth should be of damask or white linen. Set the table with gleaming silverware and use your best crystal goblets for sparkling water or a mild beer. Arrange a centerpiece of tropical fruits in a low attractive bowl interspersed with short-stemmed flowers. Spice-scented candles in silver candelabra will help create the atmosphere of the Spice Island. Attractive service plates complete the table setting.

As guests arrive for the Zanzibar dinner, put five or six whole cloves into their hands. They will look at you with surprise, but when they see that you are chewing on one, they will quickly follow suit.

The soup may be brought in from the kitchen in double-handled soup cups with an underliner and placed on the service plate. When the course is finished, the dishes, including the service plates, are removed.

Next, serve two fish croquettes on a salad plate, garnished with lemon slices studded with cloves on a bed of parsley.

Rice in an attractive bowl is spooned in a mound on dinner plates, followed by a large bowl of beef curry which each guest is invited to spoon liberally over the rice.

A glass-sectioned relish dish containing the *sambals,* or accompaniments, for a curry is passed around.

The delicate banana custard chilled in wine glasses is the dessert.

Coffee is served in the living room after dinner.

Zanzibar Hotel Luncheon Menu

SUPU YA KUKU
Chicken Soup

SAMAKAI WA KUSONGA
Fish Croquet

M'CHUZI WA NYAMA
Beef Curry

WALI
Rice

N'DIZI NO KASTAD
Banana Custard, Zanzibar Style

JISAIDIE KWA KAHAWA UKUMBINI
Please help yourself to coffee in the lounge.

Shopping List for Eight

Meats, Chicken
1 5-lb. chicken or fowl
2 lbs. boneless chuck

Dairy
½ lb. butter
6 eggs

Gourmet Shop
A good quality curry

Fruits and Vegetables
3 lbs. onions
1 small cabbage
1 lb. tomatoes
1 stalk celery
1 lemon
6 bananas
2 oranges
1 cucumber

Groceries
1 can tuna or salmon
1 pkg. bread crumbs
1 jar mango chutney
1 pkg. grated coconut
2 pkgs. no-bake custard
1 lb. shelled peanuts

SUPU YA KUKU | Chicken Soup

This chicken soup tastes better on the second day, so make it ahead of time if you can. A little curry might be added unless a curried dish is served in the same meal.

The real trick is to sauté vegetables first and then proceed to make the soup. This, by the way, is a chef's secret for making superb soups. Save the rest of the chicken (fowl) for salad for another meal. *Supu Ya Kuku* may also be made when there is leftover chicken available. In this case use four chicken bouillon cubes following above method without the fowl, but use 2 cups of diced chicken instead of 1.

Yield: 8 cups

In a 3-quart saucepan:

Sauté	½ cup	ONIONS, finely chopped
	½ cup	CABBAGE, finely chopped
	1 small	TOMATO, finely diced
	1 stalk	CELERY, finely chopped in
	2 oz.	BUTTER or MARGARINE until soft but not brown.
Add	1 5-lb.	FOWL (fat hen), cut in quarters
	2 quarts	WATER
	1 tsp.	SALT
	½ tsp.	PEPPER.

Simmer gently for 1 hour or until meat is tender.

Remove the fowl.

Cut 1 cup of the meat in ½-inch cubes and add to the soup.

Correct the Seasonings to your taste.

SAMAKI WA KUSONGA | Fish Croquettes

The fish used for making croquettes in Zanzibar is not mashed as it is here. The consistency of the fish is flaky, and the flavor of the spices of Zanzibar make this a distinctive dish. Leftover halibut, flounder, haddock, or any mild fish is excellent for croquettes. Canned tuna or salmon are also good. Make the croquettes larger if you want to make this an entrée course. The croquettes should not be deep-fat fried but lightly sautéed in butter. Don't forget the whole cloves on the lemon garnish.

Yield: 16 croquettes

In a 1-quart bowl:

Mash coarsely	1 lb.	COOKED FISH (either leftover white flaked fish or canned tuna or salmon, drained).
Add	2	EGGS lightly beaten
	1 tsp.	SALT
	1 pinch	SAFFRON
	1 Tbs.	VINEGAR
	½ tsp.	CRUSHED RED PEPPER
	1 pinch	CUMIN SEED (optional)
	3 to 4 Tbs.	BREAD CRUMBS.
Form	into 1-oz. (2-inch) croquettes.	
Place	on a bed of	
	1 cup	BREAD CRUMBS spread out on a small tray.
Press	the crumbs into the croquettes on all sides.	
Chill	in refrigerator for 1 hour.	
Sauté in	3 oz.	BUTTER or MARGARINE until golden brown on all sides.
Place	two croquettes per guest on a salad plate.	
Garnish with	2	LEMON SLICES studded with
	2 or 3	WHOLE CLOVES each.

M'CHUZI WA NYAMA | Curry of Beef Zanzibar

What a lovely curry dish this is! It is quite yellow in color, and the sauce is smooth and velvety. It is the combination of all the spices which makes this great dish. Use a good quality of curry and make it with any meat. It is frequently served with beef liver in East Africa. Try it with lamb or veal as a change.

Yield: 8 servings

In a 4-quart saucepan:

Sauté	1 cup	ONIONS, finely chopped
	1 clove	GARLIC, crushed
	1 tsp.	SALT
	1 tsp.	TURMERIC
	¼ tsp.	CHILI POWDER
	1 to 2 tsps.	CURRY POWDER in
	4 Tbs.	OIL or MARGARINE until onions are soft.
Add	2 lbs.	CHUCK of BEEF cut in ¾-inch cubes.

Sauté lightly but do not permit the meat to brown.

Add	2 cups	WATER
	4 Tbs.	LEMON JUICE.

Cover tightly and allow to simmer for 1 hour.
If the sauce appears thin, thicken it with

	2 Tbs.	CORNSTARCH dissolved in
	2 Tbs.	WATER.

Serve in a 4-quart oval bowl with RICE cooked in chicken or beef broth (allow 1 cup cooked rice per portion).

In a 6-sectioned relish dish or six small bowls:

Place	½ cup	BANANAS cut in ¼-inch dice dribbled with lemon juice.
	1 cup	FRIED ONION SLICES
	½ cup	MANGO CHUTNEY
	½ cup	GRATED or SHREDDED COCONUT
	½ cup	ORANGE SECTIONS
	½ cup	CUCUMBER in ½-inch dice.

Place the *Sambals,* or relishes, on the tables so guests may help themselves.

N'DIZI NA KASTED | Zanzibar Banana Custard

Banana custard may also be made with packaged vanilla pudding, but the "no-bake" custard requires no cooking and gives a result comparable to the custard served in Zanzibar. Pineapple, crushed or diced, may be added or substituted for the bananas and some orange sections would improve the color. Since Zanzibar is the Spice Island the strong use of cloves and cinnamon as garnish add greatly to the authenticity as well as the flavor of the dish.

Yield: 8 portions

In a 1-quart bowl:

Prepare 3 cups   NO-BAKE CUSTARD following package directions.

Slice 3   BANANAS into 8 champagne glasses.

Spoon the custard over the bananas.

Chill and permit the custard to set.

In a small bowl:

Combine 1 tsp.   CINNAMON
½ tsp.   GROUND CLOVES
¼ tsp.   NUTMEG
½ cup   SUGAR
4 Tbs.   PEANUTS finely chopped.

Sprinkle 1 heaping tablespoon of the spice mixture over each custard.

Decorate with whipped cream if desired.

BEANS AND GROUNDNUT RELISH

A typical relish that might be served at the Zanzibar dinner:

Yield: 1 quart

In a 2-quart saucepan:

Sauté ½ cup   CHOPPED ONION in
¼ cup   OIL until light brown.

Add 2   LARGE TOMATOES, thinly sliced and
2 cups   PEANUT BUTTER and sauté for 5 minutes.

Add 2 cups   COOKED PEA BEANS
1 pint   WATER.

Simmer for ½ hour or until mixture is thick.

Serve with *Ugali,* rice, yams, or sweet potatoes or as a relish with any dinner.

The Malagasy Republic

Madagascar, "The Great Red Island" as it is often called, is officially known as the Malagasy Republic. It is the fourth largest island in the world and is a land of sheer beauty. Ringed by golden beaches and date-palm trees, the interior varies from grassy plateaus, to volcanoes, and impenetrable equatorial forests. It is lush with a great variety of fruits such as mangos, grapes, peaches, pears, pineapples, avocados, and lichee nuts. All about are colorful flowers in abundance: orchids, violets, and mimosa.

Tananarive, the capital, is a picturesque city with narrow sloping streets and houses that seem to cling to the hillside. The open market, characteristic of all of Africa, is most exhilarating. There you will find the long black vanilla beans sold in little packets to be used in many ways, but mostly in flavoring fruit. A large portion of the crop (120 million vanilla beans) makes its way to the U.S.A. every year from Madagascar. Everywhere you see scallions, turnips, tomatoes, and a variety of green vegetables. And there is always plenty of fish.

The people of Madagascar are mostly Malayan Polynesian with some admixture of Indian, Arab, African, and European. Despite the variety of races one language is used throughout the island, Malagasy; the second language is French. Rice is the staple of the island and is served three times a day. Most of it is home grown.

You can recognize the influence of the French in the food, which is not as highly spiced as in most of Africa. While the curry is much like that of Malaysia, subtle and not overpowering, it is just different enough to be interesting. Most recipes call for a smidgen of red hot pepper, called *Sakay,* and it is generally served separately so that one can control the amount to taste.

The manner in which beef—*Varenga*—is treated is worthy of note. Beef is cut in small pieces, simmered until done, shredded, and then roasted until it is browned. It is suprisingly delicious and a good way to use left-over cooked beef.

How a Dinner Is Served in Malagasy

The true Malagache serves his meal, as is done in most parts of Africa, on a mat on the floor. Everything is put down at the same time—but in the cities individual plates are used and the utensil is a large spoon (no knives or forks are used).

Dinner is a simple affair. There are no preliminaries such as snacks, hors d'oeuvres, cocktails, or drinks. Guests are brought to the dining area and served directly. Today, you will find the Western influence appearing more strongly, and dining areas are being increasingly adopted.

Malagaches like their food simply prepared, flavorful, but as we have said, not highly spiced. Fruits and vegetables are utilized at their freshest, and it is not uncommon to start a meal with vegetable soup and then to serve two or three vegetables with the entrée. The beverage that goes with the meal is *Ranonapango,* a drink made by *burning* rice—yes, actually burning the rice and adding water to it. (The recipe is given on page 93.)

The entrée might very well be a chicken or fish curry, and it is usually one of the three rice meals each day. In Malagasy curries are prepared a little differently than in other countries. A Malagache curry is included in the recipe section.

The dessert is usually fruit, flavored with vanilla. Some call Madagascar the Vanilla Island as they call Zanzibar the Spice Island. The fruit is not only prepared with vanilla, but more vanilla is added to it when it is served.

Malagasy tea, their own special brand (not available here), completes a most nutritious meal.

How You Can Present a Malagasy Dinner

It might be more authentic to serve this menu on mats placed on the floor, but in the cities of Malagasy dinner would be served at a table.

For the Malagasy meal, use bright yellow tablecloths and matching napkins—on a round table, if possible, to express the feeling of friendliness. Place the napkin on a white service plate and top each napkin with a large bright flower. An iris or any flower that resembles the orchid family would be ideal but a large daisy or other flower will also serve.

The centerpiece is a bowl of fresh fruit interspersed with some of the same flowers that adorn each plate. Dishes are plain white or solid colors.

Start with the *Lasopy,* the veal vegetable purée, thick and hearty and served in earthenware bowls.

The *Varenga,* beautifully browned shredded beef, arrives in the oven-proof dish in which it was baked and is set on a trivet. A large bowl of *Vary Amin Anana,* steaming hot vegetables, and the *Lasary Voatabia,* tomato and scallion salad, are set on the table at the same time. It is not common practice to serve bread or rolls, but be sure that a large bowl of white rice is part of the dinner.

Ranonapango, the burned-rice drink would be correct to serve with the dinner, but you might want to substitute cold lemonade or ice water.

Your guests will find the dessert delicious. If you cannot obtain the fruits suggested in the *Salady Voankazo* (fresh fruits with lichee nuts), use any fruits that are available. Sugar them lightly and sprinkle pure vanilla extract over the fruit.

Serve tea or coffee in the usual manner.

The Malagache dinner is one of the easiest to prepare and to serve. And it is utterly different!

Menu from Malagasy

LASOPY
Veal Vegetable Purée

VARENGA
Roasted Shredded Beef

VARY AMIN ANANA
Rice and Greens

LASARY VOATABIA
Fresh Diced Scallions
and Tomatoes

SALADY VOANKAZO
Vanilla-spiked Fresh
Fruits with Lichee Nuts

RAVINBOAFOBY
Malagasy Tea

Shopping List for Eight

Meats	Fruits and Vegetables	Groceries
3 lbs. veal bones	3 lbs. tomatoes	1 bottle pure vanilla extract
4 lbs. boneless chuck	1 lb. potatoes	2 lbs. white rice
1 lb. soup meat	1 bunch carrots	1 box soda crackers
Gourmet shop	½ lb. turnips	
1 small can lichee nuts	½ lb. string beans	
	½ lb. mustard greens	
	½ lb. spinach	
	1 bunch watercress	
	2 bunches scallions	
	1 lemon	
	1 fresh pineapple	
	1 canteloupe	
	3 thick-skinned oranges	
	1 box strawberries	

LASOPY | Vegetable Soup

This is truly a great soup; loaded with vitamins and minerals and low in calories.

Any combination of fresh vegetables and meat bones may be used, but do not add pulses (dried beans, peas, and lentils). Nor is potato, rice, or any other starchy vegetable in the *Lasopy,* which is a true vegetable purée simply flavored with meat bones.

Yield: 8 servings

In a 4-quart pot:

Simmer	3 lbs.	VEAL BONES
	2 qts.	WATER
	2 Tbs.	SALT, for 1 hour with cover on.
Add	3	CARROTS, peeled and cut in three pieces
	1 small	TURNIP, peeled and cut in chunks
	6 to 8	SCALLIONS, cut in large pieces
	1 cup	FRESH or FROZEN STRING BEANS
	1 cup	TOMATOES, cut in quarters
	½ tsp.	BLACK PEPPER.

Simmer for about 1 hour or until vegetables are tender.

Remove the veal bones.

Put the vegetables through a sieve or vegetable mill to make a purée.

Serve thick and hot from a soup tureen into soup bowls with or without crackers.

VARENGA | Roasted Shredded Beef

Yield: 8 portions

In a 4-quart saucepan:

Combine	4 lbs.	BONELESS CHUCK, cut in 1-inch pieces.
	1 quart	WATER
	2 Tbs.	SALT
	2 cloves	GARLIC, minced finely
	1 cup	ONION, sliced.

Cover and bring to a boil; simmer gently for 2 hours or until meat can be shredded with a fork.

Add	water if necessary to keep meat at simmering point.
Shred	the meat by cutting it into thin strips. Meat should come apart easily.
Transfer	the shredded meat and sauce to a greased 9 × 12-inch baking pan (oven-proof).
Roast	at 400° for 30 minutes until it is nicely browned across the top.
Garnish with	3 or 4 PARSLEY SPRIGS and bring to the table on a trivet.
Serve	with white rice.

VARY AMIN ANANA | Rice and Vegetables

Yield: 8 portions

In a 4-quart saucepan:

Sauté	½ lb.	BONELESS CHUCK cut in ½-inch cubes in
	2 Tbs.	OIL until meat is brown on all sides.
Add	1	TOMATO cut in ½-inch chunks.
Cook		with the beef for 10 minutes.
Add	1 bunch	SCALLIONS, cut in 1-inch pieces.
	½ lb.	MUSTARD GREENS, cut in small pieces
	½ lb.	SPINACH, cut in small pieces
	1 bunch	WATERCRESS, cut in small pieces.
Sauté		stirring occasionally with cover on until vegetables soften.
Add	2 cups	WATER (or enough to cover vegetables) and
	1 cup	RICE
	1 Tbs.	SALT
	½ tsp.	PEPPER.
Cover		tightly and simmer slowly until rice is thoroughly cooked and all the liquid is absorbed.
Correct the Seasoning		to your taste.
Serve		with hot pepper *Sakay* as a relish to accompany *Lasopy.*

SAKAY | Hot Red Pepper

Yield: about 1 cup

In a 1-pint bowl:

Combine	½ cup	CRUSHED RED PEPPER
	1 Tbs.	GROUND GINGER
	2 cloves	GARLIC, crushed.
Add	4 Tbs.	OIL or enough to make a mush.
Place	1 to 2 Tbs.	*Sakay* in tiny butter dishes or pass in a bowl.

LASARY VOATABIA | Tomato and Scallion Salad

Yield: 8 small salads

In a 1-quart bowl:

Combine	1 cup	SCALLIONS, finely diced
	2 cups	TOMATOES, finely diced
	2 Tbs.	WATER
	1 tsp.	SALT
	few drops	TABASCO SAUCE.
Stir	lightly and chill.	
Serve	approximately ⅓ cup per portion in small sauce dishes.	

SALADY VOANKAZO | Fruit Compote with Lichee Nuts

Vanilla gives an unfamiliar bouquet and unusual flavor to fresh fruits.

Yield: 1 quart fruit mixture
(8 servings)

In a 2-quart glass or china bowl:

Combine	1 cup	FRESH PINEAPPLE, cut in 1-inch dice
	1 cup	CANTELOUPE, cut in ½-inch dice
	1 cup	ORANGES, peeled and very thinly sliced
	½ cup	STRAWBERRIES, sliced.

Mix	the fruits so that they are well blended.
Pour	½ cup CANNED LICHEE NUTS across top of fruit.

In a 1-pint saucepan:

Combine	½ cup	SUGAR
	½ cup	WATER
	¼ tsp.	SALT
	2 Tbs.	LEMON JUICE.

Bring	to a boil and boil hard for 1 minute.
Add	2 Tbs. PURE VANILLA EXTRACT to the syrup.
Pour	the piping hot syrup over the fruit.
Chill	in refrigerator for 1 hour.
Fill	a small cruet or sprinkler bottle with PURE VANILLA EXTRACT.
Bring	the *Salady* to the table in the bowl along with the cruet of vanilla.
Fill	individual compote dishes with the fruit.
Sprinkle	a few drops VANILLA over the fruit as it is being served.

KITOZA

This is one of the favorite foods of Malagasy. Dried beef is cut in strips and broiled over a charcoal fire. If you would like to make it, purchase round steak cut ¼-inch thick. Cut the meat in pieces about 4 inches × 2 inches, thread the strips on a fine strong cord and hang the cord up as you would a small clothesline. The meat will become quite dry in a few hours. Put the strips over a charcoal brazier so that the meat dries to a crispness but does not burn. Remove the meat immediately from the fire as it crisps. This is a great delicacy in Madagascar. It is usually eaten with a watery cornmeal mush for breakfast.

BANANA FRITTERS

These are another treat in Malagasy. They are served as a vegetable and may be added to your Malagache dinner. See recipe, page 186.

RANONAPANGO

This is the burned-rice beverage which is an important part of the meal. Malagache cooks double the quantity of rice they require for the meal. When it is cooked, they remove most of the rice from the earthenware pan. The remainder (a layer about ½-inch thick) is heated until it is burned and acquires a characteristic aroma. At that point boiling water is poured over the rice to the top of the pan. It is cooled, strained, and chilled. This beverage is used in place of water on the island.

South Africa

South Africa is a land of contrasts. The cities are as modern as any in the world and are but a few minutes from the simple kraals or villages where Bantu boys tend their cows and sheep as they have for hundreds of years. The abundant vegetation of the coastal areas gives way to flat-topped mountains and the great grass-covered tablelands known as the Veld. The natural beauty of this country is beyond description. South Africa, like Kenya, has long attracted game hunters on safari. Strict conservation measures are in effect so that a great variety of wild animals can still be seen, from the rhinoceros and elephant to the eland and wildebeest, and bird life such as parrots, pelicans, and flamingos.

The Bantu Nation represents over twenty tribes who came to South Africa from Central, East, and West Africa about three hundred years ago. Their diet consists of mealies (corn) and Kaffir corn (a grain resembling barley). Hot, spicy stews of meat and vegetables accompany the starchy porridge.

The White Nation, which speaks English and Afrikaans, first settled in Africa in the 17th century, coming mainly from England and Holland. Germans and Portuguese also formed colonies, and all of these Europeans have brought with them their own foods and adapted them to the native foods. The English brought their meat pies, biscuits, and puddings; the Germans, their knowledge of pastries and cakes; the Dutch, the marvelous rice dishes from Indonesia. Such dishes as *Sosaties, Bobotie, Koesisters, Bredies,* Chutney, now typically South African, were brought by the Malays who introduced their spices and curries.

The result is a cuisine with interesting combinations of Eastern and

Western foods. Add to these the perennial South African delicacy Rock Lobster Tail with wine from the Cape and there is something to please everyone.

How Dinner Is Served in South Africa

Your invitation might come from a Bantu or from an Afrikaaner. Should you be asked to visit the circular huts in the kraals of any of the Bantu tribes as an "honored" guest, you would be treated with the same hospitality as you will find in all of Africa. Food in large earthenware pots would be spread out on mats on the floor. The menu would probably consist of *Putu,* the thick cornmeal porridge made from mealies, topped with a hot spicy stew and followed by homemade beer. It is a simple repast but no less enjoyable than the spread of delicacies presented by the Afrikaaner.

In the home of the Afrikaaner hospitality means "lots of food." The table is set with a white tablecloth. In the center is a huge bowl of fruit, and cruets of vinegar and Worcestershire sauce, and salt- and pepper-shakers. Brightly polished silverware and china dishes, probably from England, adorn the table. Wines are from the Cape of South Africa.

Dinner may start with a hearty soup or fish. Rock Lobster Tail might be served as an appetizer or an entrée. Or dishes like Green Bean *Bredie,* a stew made with "a thick rib of mutton" cooked with potatoes and string beans might be served. When South Africans really wish to give their friends a treat they prepare their special version of Chicken Pie made with chicken, ham or bacon, and hard-boiled eggs. *Bitlong,* long pieces of meat salted and dried, might be an hors d'oeuvre or a snack served with bread and butter. Mealies in some form are a must whether as a vegetable, a bread, a soufflé, or in a soup.

A hostess would probably serve *Sosaties,* piping hot with the sauce even hotter. These are the South African version of brochettes. They are always served with crisp biscuits. *Bobotie,* chopped or minced beef in a curry, is a typical dish and your hostess will make it for you if you request it. South Africans love to cook.

Desserts may be either fruits and cookies or a rich pudding or cake.

African coffee or English tea complete the dinner.

You may be handed a tall glass of cool *Mechow.* It is a drink made from cornmeal which has been prepared as a thin gruel and permitted to ferment with a little sugar. It stands for two or three days, then is stirred until smooth.

How You Can Present a South African Dinner

Your South African dinner should be formal. Use a crisp white damask tablecloth and matching napkins. Set the table with bone-china dishes (or your best) and gleaming silverware. Make a centerpiece of flowers or fruits and flowers in a low arrangement. Silver candlesticks with white candles are appropriate. Crystal water glasses and wine glasses complete the setting.

Plan to serve at least two kinds of wine with this dinner. Do not plan to serve hors d'oeuvres since the food is hearty and filling.

Start with the small stuffed rock lobster tails on small dishes. You might serve a dry white Chablis with this course.

The *Sosaties* with the tips of the skewers piercing a head of cabbage make an attractive dish. Place the cabbage on a wooden platter and garnish with tomato slices. The yellow rice and the string-bean salad should be served first, then followed with the *Sosatie*. A good rosé wine is ideal for this course.

Pass the Mealie Bread, cut in small slices or squares, from a bread plate covered with a cloth napkin. Serve whipped butter in an attractive bowl or crock. Don't forget the cruets of vinegar and Worcestershire sauce and the salt and pepper.

After the dinner, serve slices of honeydew, canteloupe, or watermelon. *Soetkoekies,* spice cookies, may be served with freshly made coffee at this time or later in the evening.

Menu from South Africa

SOUTH AFRICAN ROCK LOBSTER TAIL
Appetizer

SOSATIES
Lamb and Apricots on
a Skewer

YELLOW RICE AND RAISINS   **MEALIE BREAD**   **GREEN BEAN SALAD**

MELON SLICES

and

SOETKOEKIES
Traditional Spice
Cookies

SOUTH AFRICAN RED BUSH TEA

Shopping List for Eight

Meat and Fish
2 lbs. lamb for skewers
1 lb. fat pork
8 3-oz. South African
   rock lobsters

Dairy
½ lb. butter
6 eggs
1 quart milk

Beverages
Sherry
red wine
rosé wine

Fruits and Vegetables
1 lb. Spanish onions
2 lbs. fresh string
   beans
2 lemons
1 large honeydew
   melon
1 head lettuce
1 stalk celery
1 bunch parsley

Groceries
2 lbs. all-purpose flour
1 lb. brown sugar
1 packet slivered
   almonds
1 box cream of tartar
1 package biscuit mix
1 #2 can kernel corn
1 small jar apricot
   jam
1 lb. dried apricots
1 lb. rice
1 box raisins
1 small jar small
   stuffed olives
1 pint mayonnaise
1 can pimientos
1 can black olives
1 pint salad oil
1 jar mango chutney

SOUTH AFRICAN ROCK LOBSTER TAIL | Appetizer

Yield: 8 portions

Thaw	8 3-ounce	AFRICAN ROCK LOBSTER TAILS.
		In a 4-quart saucepan:
Cover		LOBSTER TAILS with warm water from tap.
Add	1 tsp.	SALT and
	½	LEMON cut in wedges. Cover.
Simmer		slowly for 5 minutes.
Turn		off the flame, and allow to stand in the water for 30 minutes.
Cool		and drain.
Cut		around the edge of the underside of the shell to remove meat and cut meat in ½-inch pieces.
Place		in a 2-quart bowl.
Add	1 cup	CELERY in ½-inch dice
	½ cup	HONEYDEW MELON in ½-inch dice
	½ cup	MAYONNAISE blended with
	1 tsp.	CURRY POWDER
	1 tsp.	PAPRIKA and
	1 tsp.	GROUND GINGER.
Blend		together and replace mixture in the shells, piling it high.
Garnish with	1 strip	PIMIENTO, ½-inch wide and
	2	BLACK OLIVES, one on each side of each lobster.
Shred	½ head	LETTUCE.
Arrange		small beds of lettuce on 6-inch plates.
Place	1	LOBSTER on each lettuce bed with
	1	LEMON WEDGE at the side.

SOSATIES | Lamb and Apricots on Skewers

South Africans marinate meat for *Sosaties* two or three days. But we impatient Americans may settle for one to two days because our meat is more tender. The combination of lamb, fatty pork, and apricots spread across yellow rice is really great.

Yield: 8 skewers

Order	2 lbs.	LAMB cut in 1-inch cubes for skewers and
	1 lb.	FAT PORK cut in ½-inch cubes, from your butcher.
Rub	a 6-quart china or glass bowl with garlic.	
Sprinkle	the lamb and fatty pork with salt and pepper and place in bowl.	

In a 2-quart saucepan:

Sauté	1 cup	ONIONS, finely chopped
	1 Tbs.	CURRY POWDER
	1 clove	GARLIC, minced, in
	4 Tbs.	OIL until golden brown.
Add	2 Tbs.	SUGAR
	2 cups	WHITE VINEGAR
	2 Tbs.	APRICOT JAM
	2 Tbs.	CORNSTARCH dissolved in
	2 Tbs.	RED WINE.

Simmer   stirring constantly until mixture thickens slightly and clears (about 3 minutes).

Cool   and blend it through the meat until well combined.

Allow   to marinate in sauce for 1 to 2 days.

In a 1-quart bowl:

Marinate	½ lb.	DRIED APRICOTS in
	½ cup	SHERRY (sweet or dry) overnight.

Drain   meat from sauce.

Thread   lamb, pork, and apricots alternately on 9- to 10-inch bamboo or metal skewers.

Grill   over charcoal, or under broiler brushed with oil, until browned on all sides.

Heat   the above sauce until piping hot and serve separately with yellow rice and chutney.

MEALIE BREAD

Of course, this recipe is an adaptation of the Green Mealie Bread served in South Africa. Mealies are the African version of our corn. Mealie cobs are plunged into boiling water, cooled, and the corn stripped from the cobs and finely chopped. Sugar, salt, baking powder, milk, and sometimes an egg are added (but no flour), and the mixture is baked or steamed. It is turned out of the pan like a bread and sliced. The closest substitute would be our sweet succulent corn baked into a biscuit dough.

Yield: 9-inch square bread pan

In a 2-quart bowl:

Mix	2 cups	BISCUIT MIX with
	1 cup	CREAMED CORN (canned) and
	2 Tbs.	SUGAR.
Add	1	EGG and
	½ cup	MILK to form a soft dough.
Spread	out in greased 9-inch baking pan.	
Spread	2 oz.	MELTED BUTTER over the bread.
Bake	at 400° for 20 minutes until done.	
Cut	into squares and serve warm with butter.	

VETKOEK | Fried Bread

The above Mealie Bread (with or without the corn) may be dropped by teaspoonfuls in ½ inch of hot frying oil or shortening, flattened with a spoon as it is frying, and turned over to assure uniform browning. These tiny fried "breads" are served at *Braaivleis* (South African barbecues) with jam or syrup.

YELLOW RICE WITH RAISINS

Yield: 8 large portions

In a 3-quart saucepan:

Bring	6 cups	WATER to a boil.
Add	¼ cup	SUGAR
	1 tsp.	TURMERIC (or few drops of yellow vegetable coloring)

1 Tbs.	SALT	
1 Tbs.	BUTTER	
1 stick	CINNAMON (or 1 tsp. ground)	
1 cup	RAISINS	
1 tsp.	LEMON RIND.	

Bring to a rapid boil.

Add 2 cups   WHITE RICE.

Cover and cook for 20 minutes or until rice is tender and all the water is absorbed.

GREEN BEAN SALAD

Yield: 8 portions

In a 2-quart saucepan:

Simmer 2 lbs.   FRESH WHOLE STRING BEANS trimmed at ends in boiling salted water to cover until tender.

In a 3-quart bowl:

Combine
1 cup	SWEET WHITE ONIONS, very thinly sliced
½ cup	SALAD OIL
4 Tbs.	LEMON JUICE
1 tsp.	SALT
½ tsp.	FRESHLY GROUND PEPPER
¼ cup	SLICED STUFFED OLIVES.

Drain the string beans and, while still hot, toss quickly with onion mixture.

Chill thoroughly.

Serve as a vegetable without lettuce.

SOETKOEKIES | Spice Cookies

South Africans speak glowingly of *Soetkoekies* and the cookie jar. They get misty eyed with nostalgia for the days when grandmother's pantry was laden with home bottled fruits and jams, and wonderful smells of mingled spices wafted from her kitchen. Best of all were the cookies kept in a bottomless jar which she served with freshly brewed coffee.

Yield: About 3 dozen cookies

In a 4-quart bowl:

Mix	2 lbs.	ALL-PURPOSE FLOUR
	½ tsp.	BAKING SODA
	½ tsp.	CREAM OF TARTAR
	1 tsp.	CINNAMON
	½ tsp.	GROUND GINGER
	½ tsp.	GROUND NUTMEG
	1 cup	BROWN SUGAR
	4 oz.	CHOPPED ALMONDS.
Cut in	½ cup	BUTTER or MARGARINE as for pie crust.
Add	2	EGGS lightly beaten
	¼ cup	RED WINE.

Knead together and form into a roll two inches thick.

Wrap in wax paper and refrigerate over night.

Cut in ⅛-inch slices with a sharp knife.

Brush with 1 egg white, beaten.

Bake at 400° on a greased cookie sheet for 10 to 12 minutes until golden brown.

Remove with a spatula and place on rack to cool.

In South Africa Red Bush Tea is served. This is actually English tea as we know it—strong, pungent, and served very fresh. Indian or Chinese tea is also popular and may be used. If you decide to serve coffee, prepare it only moments before serving so that the aroma can be enjoyed with the cookies.

Liberia

Liberia, its name derived from the Latin *liber,* meaning "free," was founded by freed American slaves in the early nineteenth century. The most important city is Monrovia and was named in honor of President Monroe, who held office at the time the Republic was officially established. Red, white, and blue mailboxes, American currency, and the widespread use of English bespeak the American influence, and it is not unlike visiting part of our own country in the summertime.

Liberia is a delightful country. The waterfront market of Monrovia teems with activity, particularly in the early morning hours. Here one sees both American and African influences in the dress of the Liberians. Women may effect Western dress or wear long cotton skirts in startling colors with bandannas loosely wrapped around their heads. Smiling and friendly, they made us feel most welcome.

Cassava, addoes, tiny hot red peppers, sweet potatoes, yams, and green bananas dominate the market, but there are also collard greens, cabbage, eggplant, okra, coconut, and fresh ginger. The staple food is rice, which is eaten twice a day in most households.

Tiny roadside restaurants are called "Cook Shops" and feature Jollof Rice along with an assortment of stews. As in Ghana, cooking is done outdoors on the ubiquitous three-stone hearth. Many of these, such as Roseline's, a favorite of Liberian government officials, offer excellent fare. You'll find dishes like cabbage cooked with bacon and pigs' feet, sweet-potato leaves with fish, palm nuts with shrimp in fish or chicken stock, and dried Norwegian fish. Check Rice, a delightful combination of rice and platto leaves or okra, is a popular dish. Goat Soup is the national soup and is served at every important state function.

Liberians love sweet desserts and American pastries such as sweet-potato pie, coconut pie, and pumpkin pie. Peanuts are used in cookies and desserts of all kinds. Liberian rice bread made with mashed bananas is a great delicacy. Ginger beer and palm wine are the preferred beverages. Liberian coffee is excellent.

The greeting of one Liberian to another is unusual, and you might greet your guests this way at your Liberian dinner. When shaking hands you grasp the middle finger of your friend's right hand between your thumb and third finger and bring it up quickly with a snap. The custom had its origin in the days of slavery when it was not uncommon for a slave owner to break the finger of his slave's hand to indicate bondage. When the freed slaves colonized Liberia, they began this ritualistic greeting as a "sign" of their freedom.

How a Dinner Is Served in Liberia

A feeling of good fellowship and relaxation is reflected at a Liberian table. When you are a guest in a Liberian home, you are overwhelmed by the number of dishes spread before you. You will find **Dumboy** and *Foo-foo* made from cassava and served with Palm Butter, *Palava Sauce,* a meat stew made with a spinach-like leaves (this sauce and other soups, sauces, and stews all have a similar consistency corresponding to our stews). Then there might be Liberia's "Country Chop," probably their best-known dish, consisting of meats, fish, and greens fried in palm oil. There will also be dishes like fish cooked in coconut cream, fried plantains, Jollof Rice, Beef Internal Soup, all set on the table at the same time. Liberian rice bread and sweet-potato pone might also grace the table, with pitchers of ginger beer.

The hostess, dressed in a long, strikingly colorful skirt, a handsome blouse, and a huge bandanna, spends a great deal of time preparing this dinner. Then she sets all of the bowls on the table and sits down. She remains seated until the dinner is completely finished.

Food is eaten with the fingers by many Africans, but the American influence in Liberia is very strong, and most hostesses set the tables with plates and glasses, both turned over with the napkin resting on the inverted plate.

Fruits may be served later in the evening. In Monrovia we had sumptuous mangos with cloves, a perfect ending to a hearty meal.

How You Can Present a Liberian Dinner

For your Liberian dinner, use a plain white or striped tablecloth with matching napkins. No centerpiece is necessary, but arrange colorful bowls and platters in a long row in the center of the table if it is an oblong one. In this case no one sits at each end of the table, because there will be a lot of passing of dishes.

When setting the table, turn the plates upside down so as to allow each guest to turn up his plate himself. Place the napkins on the tops of the overturned plates. Also, turn down the beer glasses. Everything will be eaten from one dinner plate. Place the soup in a tureen and place small soup bowls in front of it. Guests are asked to help themselves.

It's fun to be a hostess for a Liberian dinner. Everything goes on the table at once. There may be more preparation time required, to be sure, but once finished, appetizer, soup, entrées, vegetables, desserts, and beverages are all served in bowls and platters and the hostess can then sit with her guests and enjoy herself. No dishes are removed until the dinner is over.

The ginger beer, ice cold in a glass pitcher, is served right along with the dinner.

Coffee is not generally served except at state functions; a pity as the Liberian home-grown coffee is so delicious. The ginger beer is well worth the effort it takes to make it. If you serve it, be warned—it has quite a kick.

Menu from Liberia

BEEF INTERNAL SOUP

JOLLOF RICE

MONROVIAN COLLARDS AND CABBAGE

SWEET POTATO PONE

GINGER BEER

Shopping List for Eight

Meat, Fish, Poultry	Fruits and Vegetables	Groceries
1 lb. beef for stew	2 lbs. fresh tomatoes	3 6-oz. cans tomato
1 3-lb. chicken	5 lbs. yellow onions	paste
(Jollof Rice)	1 bunch collard greens	1 package yeast
½ lb. tripe (optional)	2 lbs. cabbage	1 quart vegetable oil
½ lb. dried cod	3 lbs. sweet potatoes	2 lbs. white rice
1 lb. smoked fish	1 lb. green peppers	1 package instant
½ lb. bacon	1 fresh coconut	mashed potatoes
Dairy	2 pineapples	1 16-oz. can whole
1 lb. butter	1 lb. fresh ginger	tomatoes
		1 jar tiny hot peppers
		1 quart molasses

BEEF INTERNAL SOUP

Check dried codfish for saltiness. If very salty it may need to be soaked overnight, in which case eliminate salt from recipe.

Liberian soups are unlike most soup dishes and are often a combination of meats, fish, and vegetables ultimately combined in one pot. With less water they may be served as main dishes. Other vegetables such as okra and string beans may be added.

Yield: 3 quarts soup

In a 1-gallon pot :

Combine
1 lb.	STEW BEEF, cut in ½-inch dice
½ lb.	TRIPE, cut in small pieces (optional)
1 6-oz. can	TOMATO PASTE
1 Tbs.	SALT
1 tsp.	COARSE RED PEPPER
1 tsp.	BLACK PEPPER
½ lb.	FRESH TOMATOES, cut in ½-inch squares
1 quart	WATER.

Simmer for one hour or until meat is tender.

In another 1-gallon pot:

Combine
½ lb.	ONIONS, thinly sliced
½ lb.	DRIED CODFISH, cut in small pieces, in
2 quarts	WATER.

Simmer until fish is tender.

Combine fish and meat and simmer slowly for 20 minutes.

Debone 1 large SMOKED FISH (herring, mackerel, whitefish, etc.).

Add to soup and cook 10 minutes longer.

Correct the Seasonings to your taste.

Serve with rice or *Foo-foo.*

JOLLOF RICE

Jollof Rice is served with variations in many countries of West Africa. In Liberia pigs' feet are used with salt pork and bacon as well as with chicken. This dish may be made from scratch with fresh chicken pieces, alone or in combination, but it is also an excellent dish for leftover chicken, veal, turkey, tongue, ham, bacon, etc.

Yield: 8 portions

In a 10-inch skillet:

Sauté   2 lbs.   COOKED MEATS (such as chicken, bacon, shrimp, smoked pork) cut in 1-inch chunks in
½ cup   VEGETABLE OIL until slightly brown.

In a 4-quart kettle:

Sauté   ½ cup   YELLOW ONIONS, finely chopped
½ cup   GREEN PEPPERS, finely chopped
½ tsp.   GROUND GINGER (optional), in
¼ cup   VEGETABLE OIL until onions are soft.

Add   1 16-oz.
can   WHOLE TOMATOES (2 cups).

Simmer for 5 minutes.

Add   2 6-oz.
cans   TOMATO PASTE
2 quarts   WATER
1 Tbs.   SALT
½ tsp.   BLACK PEPPER
½ tsp.   THYME
1 tsp.   CRUSHED RED PEPPER.

Add   the cooked meat and simmer 20 minutes longer.

In a 2-quart saucepan:

Cook   2 cups   WHITE RICE in
5 cups   CHICKEN STOCK or WATER until tender.

**Correct the
Seasonings** with salt, pepper, etc.

Combine the sauce of the meat with the rice.

Pour   the Jollof Rice in a deep bowl, arranging the meat in the center.

MONROVIAN COLLARDS AND CABBAGE

If collard greens are not available, use 2 lbs. spinach instead, in which case cut cooking time to 10 minutes.

Yield: 8 portions

In a 4-quart saucepan:

Combine
1 bunch	COLLARD GREENS, washed and cut in small pieces
½ lb.	BACON, cut in 1- to 2-inches pieces*
1 large	ONION, sliced
1 Tbs.	SALT
1 Tbs.	CRUSHED RED PEPPER
1 tsp.	BLACK PEPPER and
1 quart	WATER.

Simmer gently for 30 minutes.

Add
2 lbs.	CABBAGE cut into 8 wedges and
1 oz.	BUTTER or OIL.

Cook for 15 minutes or longer until vegetables are tender.

Correct the Seasoning to your taste.

Strain before serving if water has not been absorbed.

Serve in a 2-quart bowl.

LIBERIAN SWEET POTATO PONE

Yield: 9-inch square potato pone

In a 3-quart saucepan:

Combine
3 cups	GRATED RAW SWEET POTATOES
1 cup	MOLASSES OR DARK CANE SYRUP
2 tsp.	GROUND GINGER
2 tsp.	BAKING POWDER
1 tsp.	SALT
⅓ cup	VEGETABLE OIL.

* Ham hocks previously cooked may be substituted for bacon, but save the water in which ham hocks were cooked to use as the liquid for the recipe.

Simmer	slowly, stirring constantly, for 10 minutes.
Pour	into well-greased 9-inch baking pan.
Bake	at 325° for 30 minutes, stirring up every 5 minutes for the first 20 minutes.
Smooth	down the top and allow to brown.
Cut	into squares and serve either hot or cold.

GINGER BEER

Ginger beer may be diluted with water or extra sugar, or ginger may be added to obtain desired taste. Liberians make the ginger beer with the peelings of pineapple only.

Yield: more than 2½ gallons

Chop	1 lb.	FRESH GINGER finely, and then beat to a powder.
Add	2	FRESH PINEAPPLES unpeeled and cut in chunks.
Pour	2 gallons	BOILING WATER over and allow to cool to lukewarm.
Add	2 tsp.	YEAST dissolved in ½ cup of lukewarm water.
Allow	to stand overnight covered.	
Add	3½ cups	MOLASSES on the following day.
Chill	and strain.	Bottle tightly and refrigerate.

FRIED PLANTAINS

These will make a very authentic addition to your dinner, and will add to the presentation. Cut four plantains in half lengthwise and then crosswise into six uniform pieces. Sauté them quickly in a quarter of an inch of hot oil in a sauté pan. Use green bananas if plantains are not available.

• Other dishes in the recipe section which go well with this dinner are Mrs. Dukuly's Fresh White Fish in Coconut Cream (page 154), Palaver Sauce (page 180), and if you can make the Liberian Rice Bread (page 205), it will be quite an added attraction.

• Coconut Pie is quite a favorite in Liberia. You might want to serve it later in the evening. See Mrs. Spear's (of Monrovia) famous Coconut Pie in the dessert section (page 216).

STEWED MANGOS WITH CLOVES

A simple fruit dessert might be added to the dinner or served later in the evening. You can make this with fresh or canned (yellow cling) peaches or apricots if mangos are not available. Use two 24-oz. cans of peaches or apricots for eight servings.

In a 1-quart saucepan:

Place	4 large	MANGOS peeled and cut in large pieces.
Add	1 cup	SYRUP from a can of peaches and
	6	WHOLE CLOVES.
Simmer	for 15 minutes or until mangos are tender.	
Spear	some of the pieces with a few cloves.	
Cool	and serve in compote dishes.	

Ghana

Ghana is a delightful country, and a visitor there receives a warm and friendly welcome. This tiny country on the West Coast of Africa is the world's largest exporter of cocoa. English is widely spoken, and the British influence is generally much in evidence. Africans who once drank palm wine, coconut milk, and corn beer now often drink tea. It is interesting that they have adopted the use of the word tea as a general word for "beverage" with connotations of relaxation and congeniality. Tea is called by them Tea-Tea; coffee, Coffee-Tea, and similarly there are Cocoa-Tea, Ovaltine-Tea, Horlicke-Tea, etc. There is also African-Tea, a mixture of sugar and water which has never been near a tea leaf!

The food of Ghana is similar to that in other countries of West Africa. The potato-like root, cassava, is grated to make *Gari*, is cooked to make *Foo-foo*, and is often combined with mashed plantains. *Kenkey* is an interesting dish of fermented corn dough, rolled inside leaves, and steamed. Of course there are foods with which we are unfamiliar. *Kononmire* are the big green leaves from the cocoyam. Palm nuts are the little red fruit of the palm tree, and *Agusi* are the small melon seeds which are ground and used as a flour.

It is amusing that as we were adapting to these unfamiliar foods, we came across these handy hints for foreigners attempting to use African foods in their traditional recipes.

Pawpaw, boiled and mashed, makes good pumpkin pie filling.
Green mangos make an apple pie. Ripe mangos a peach pie. Potato chips may be made from cassava, plantain or yam sliced thin and quickly fried.

How a Dinner Is Served in Ghana

One morning in the market at Accra, we suddenly came upon a restaurant; pots loaded with food bubbling away on the three-stone hearth in the noonday sun filled the air with a wonderful aroma. A young man nearby was rhythmically pounding cassava in a wooden bowl. The young woman next to him sat stirring the contents and adding mashed plantains each time the man raised his pestle. Other young people were hard at work preparing the luncheon meal.

The youngest of this group was a girl of about eighteen who was the manager and apparently the taster. She was very pleased when we made known our interest in what she was making. The soup she was stirring and frequently tasting was *Nkrakra Soup,* pronounced En-kra-kra, a light soup. The dark soup in another pot was made with peanuts. We were her first customers. She ushered us indoors, into a tiny room just large enough to seat six, and served us small portions from five of the dishes she was making. Of course we asked her for her recipes. This is how she described her recipe for light soup:

"Take   2 pence onions
3 shillings 2 pence green peppers
4 shillings garden eggs (a vegetable like eggplant)
9 pence okra
2 shillings tomatoes
5 shillings 3 pence cut meat
2 pence beans.

Cover with water. Add herbs, and a little hot pepper. Cook for two hours."

The dish was very hot but very good. This sort of dish is what a Ghanaian might make his main meal.

How You Can Present a Ghanaian Dinner

When you have a yen to express real friendliness, invite your guests (especially a group of women) to a luncheon, Ghanaian style. Everyone sits around chatting like magpies and thoroughly enjoying the delightful repast. The dishes are examined and discussed and recipes are exchanged. You will be asked to write the recipes out for the unusual menu you are serving.

Such was the luncheon we will never forget in Accra under the graceful sponsorship of Miss Angela Christian of the Health Ministry of Ghana, at the home of Alberta Ollenku. Each dish was prepared by a different woman active in affairs of state and each an excellent cook. Nowhere can there be greater rapport than when women find common ground exchanging food ideas.

Keep the mood light and friendly for your Ghanaian luncheon. Use colorful cotton cloths and bright napkins to contrast with white china plates and bowls and a simple chafing dish to keep the stew hot. Set the table as you would for a festive luncheon, with your best silverware and water glasses. Fresh flowers on the table in a low bouquet and lots of greenery around the room will brighten the scene.

Serve the Groundnut Soup first in little bowls. It should be served cold if the weather is warm. Bring in the steaming dish of Eggplant Stew, a bowl of white rice, and a bowl filled with Yam Balls. It may appear starchy but the combination is most compatible. You might want a salad. If so, see page 197. To keep the mood informal, everyone helps himself. Have a pitcher of lemonade, orangeade, or fruit drink on the table.

Dessert is a Fool, refrigerated in champagne glasses and served with a small plate as underliner. Sweet biscuits or wafers accompany the Fool. Tea is the usual beverage, but if you can get African coffee, it will add a plus to your luncheon.

- Salads are not popular in Ghana or in West Africa, but a dark green salad of chopped spinach leaves topped with crushed, crisp bacon, and a mild French dressing is suggested to round out the Ghanaian lunch. (2 lbs. spinach and 2 to 3 strips of crisp bacon chopped fine are all that are needed. Add them to your market list.)

- *Kelewele* is made of plantain chips seasoned with ginger and pepper and fried in hot oil. It makes a fine hors d'oeuvre and is easy to fix. Merely slice plantains or green bananas as thinly as possible and sprinkle with ginger and pepper before frying.

- As a cocktail you might serve a Pawpaw Paradise. See beverage section (page 222). Pawpaw is so good you will not mind if it is served again for dessert.

Menu from Ghana

GROUNDNUT SOUP

FROI
Fish and Shrimp in An Eggplant Stew

YAM BALLS

PAWPAW FOOL

FRUIT ADE

TEA   **COFFEE**

Shopping List for Eight

Meat, Fish, Poultry
1 5½- to 6-lb. fowl or
   chicken
2 lbs. filet of sole or
   flounder
1 lb. shrimp (20 to 25)

Dairy
6 eggs
½ pint heavy cream

Beverages
dry white wine
   (optional)

Vegetables and Fruits
3 lbs. yellow onions
1 lb. green peppers
½ lb. fresh tomatoes
2 large eggplants
3 lbs. yams or sweets
2 lemons
2 papayas or yellow
   melons
1 lb. carrots

Groceries
1 6-oz. can tomato
   paste
½ lb. peanut butter
2 lbs. white rice
2 cans evaporated milk
1 pkg. cornflake
   crumbs
1 pkt. candied fruit
½ pint salad oil
1 pkg. sweet biscuits
   or wafers

GROUNDNUT SOUP | Peanut Soup

Groundnut Soup may be served hot or cold. If it is served cold, it should be thoroughly chilled.

Yield: 2-3 quarts

In a 6-quart pot:

Place	1	LITTLE FAT HEN (5½ to 6 lbs.), cut in quarters and then in eighths
	2 medium	ONIONS, whole, peeled
	4	CARROTS, whole, peeled
	1 Tbs.	SALT
	½ tsp.	BLACK PEPPER
	2 quarts	WATER.
Cover		and simmer gently until chicken is done—about 45 minutes.
Remove		the chicken, onions, and carrots.
Add	6-oz. can	TOMATO PASTE to the stock, and
	8-oz.	PEANUT BUTTER (blend both tomato paste and peanut butter with a little stock and return to the pot)
	¼ tsp.	CAYENNE PEPPER
	¼ tsp.	CRUSHED RED PEPPER.
Cook		slowly until oil rises to the top, about twenty minutes.
Skim		off the oil.
Add	¼ cup	DRY WHITE WINE (optional)
Correct the Seasoning		to your taste.

Groundnut Stew

Save the chicken, onions, and carrots for the following day and serve your family Groundnut Stew. Cut up the chicken, onions, and carrots and add leftover Groundnut Soup (if any) to make a stew which is served with rice. Or you may want to cook up sweet potatoes and add to the dish.

Groundnut Sauce

Thicken Groundnut Soup with flour to make a most delicate sauce which can be used with cooked bananas, plantains, and yams. As a change pour this sauce over yam balls.

FROI | Eggplant Stew

Froi is another dish with hundreds of variations. Mrs. Essie Akwei of Accra makes *Froi* with beef, smoked fish, and okra. In some recipes the fish is flaked or ground. The most attractive way to serve *Froi* is to leave the fish whole and garnish it with shrimp.

If you like eggplant this is probably one of the most delicious ways to serve it. Eggplant and fish make a divine combination.

Yield: 8 portions

In a 4-quart saucepan:

Combine	2 lbs.	EGGPLANT (2 large), peeled and cut in chunks
	½ cup	ONIONS, coarsely chopped
	½ cup	GREEN PEPPERS, coarsely chopped
	½ lb.	FRESH TOMATOES, in large pieces
	1 pint	WATER
	1 Tbs.	SALT
	1 tsp.	CRUSHED RED PEPPER
	1 tsp.	BLACK PEPPER.

Cover tightly and simmer until tender.

Put through a food mill and grind to a smooth paste.

In a 6-quart metal casserole or Dutch oven:

Sauté	1 cup	ONIONS coarsely chopped in
	3 Tbs.	OIL until soft but not brown.

Spread the puréed vegetables uniformly over the onions.

Arrange	2 lbs.	FILET OF SOLE (or any flat fish) over vegetables, and
	1 lb.	SEAFOOD (such as shrimp, crabmeat, or lobster) over the fish.

Pour 1 cup WATER around the edges.

Cover tightly and simmer or bake at 350° for 30 minutes.

Uncover and if it is watery place on low flame until excess water evaporates.

Serve directly from pan with rice, mashed yams, or boiled plantains.

YAM BALLS

Yield: 16 2-inch balls

In a 3-quart saucepan:

Cook 3 lbs. FRESH YAMS in boiling salted water until tender.

Drain and cool, peel, and mash until smooth.

Add
3 medium	EGGS
½ cup	EVAPORATED MILK
2 Tbs.	ONION, finely chopped
¼ tsp.	GARLIC POWDER
1 tsp.	SALT
4 Tbs.	FLOUR.

Chill mixture for 1 hour until thoroughly cold.

Form into 2-inch balls, and place on a tray.

Deep-Fat Fry at 360° for about 3 minutes or until golden brown.

Serve plain as a vegetable or with a sauce of thickened Groundnut Soup.

Yam Balls may also be dipped in seasoned flour, beaten egg, and then in bread crumbs or cornflake crumbs. This improves their appearance and gives them a crispy crust.

You may also use half white potatoes and half yams or sweet potatoes, a combination which results in a texture very much like the yam balls in Ghana.

For an interesting change of pace, combine mashed sardines, or finely chopped cooked meat, or flaked fish with the yams. These can be formed into patties and sautéed as a luncheon dish.

PAWPAW FOOL

A Fool is really a sieved fruit blended into a custard. We enjoyed this variation made by Patience A. Kotel at the home of Mrs. Alberta Ollenku and found it so easy to make that we selected it as the dessert for Ghana. Mrs. Kotel also made a Sour Sop Cream which was superb, but we are not lucky enough to have sour sop (a delectable fruit) available to us. Our variation would probably be made with crushed pineapple or bananas. The recipe is the same as below except that the fruit is blended first with condensed milk (½ cup) and the fruit mixture is frozen in freezer trays. Other recipes for making Fools are in the dessert section of Part III.

Yield: 1 quart

In a 2-quart saucepan:

Immerse	1 14-oz can	EVAPORATED MILK in WATER and boil for 20 minutes.
Chill		thoroughly for several hours, with a 2-quart bowl and egg beater.
Whip		the chilled milk in the cold bowl using the cold egg beater
Add	¼ cup ½ cup	LEMON JUICE and SUGAR.
Fold in	3 cups	PAPAYA or YELLOW MELON (very ripe) cut in tiny dice.
Pile		high in sundae or champagne glasses.
Garnish		with WHIPPED CREAM topped with CANDIED FRUIT cut in small pieces.
Chill		thoroughly before serving.
Serve		with SWEET BISCUITS or WAFERS.

• In a little restaurant in Accra called The Ebony we again sampled many Ghanaian dishes, including Jollof Rice, Boiled Plantains, Palaver Sauce, etc. When we requested dessert, our waiter brought a Jam Tart he called *Apitzi.*

It was made like this:

1 slice of bread was spread with strawberry (or any red) jam with a big blob of the jam in the center. It was topped with another slice of bread. The outside of the bread was brushed with oil (you use butter) and put into a waffle iron which sealed the ends and browned the bread.

They sold like hot cakes from their little shop at the restaurant entrance— at about ten American cents each.

PART II

AN AFRICAN BUFFET

An African Buffet

An African buffet is your opportunity to let your imagination run riot. This menu is ideal for entertaining about twenty-five people and is very simple to prepare.

Buy any bright inexpensive African fabric by the yard for your tablecloths and napkins—a bold print or vivid stripe—whatever seems inviting and lively. For the centerpiece you might use a hand of bananas surrounded by coconuts, avocados, mangos, fresh pineapple in pieces, cucumbers, eggplants, and whole peanuts. Spread out blueberry or lemon leaves on the cloth and place flowers among them. Or put your ingenuity to work with other arrangements of fruits, leaves, nuts, or raw vegetables. Any natural foliage readily available can be used on the table and in arrangements around the room.

If you choose to have the soup, which is optional, serve it at the tables as a first course before your guests go to the buffet. The soup must be very cold.

The cold buffet consists of Shrimp Trees and Avocado Mousse.

The hot buffet includes a Roast Beef Round, as it gives the buffet an elegant touch. Serve the Chicken Moamba in a 2-quart chafing dish surrounded by the small dishes of garnishes.

The Jungle Salad may be placed on the buffet table or served in individual wooden bowls directly to the guests at the tables.

Plan to have the dishes removed from the tables and the dessert and coffee served to the guests.

Menu for an African Buffet

COLD CUCUMBER SOUP

SHRIMP TREES WITH PILLI-PILLI SAUCE

AVOCADO MOUSSE

RHODESIAN MELON MOLD

ROAST BEEF ROUND

CHICKEN MOAMBA

SWEET POTATO   SPINACH

RICE BUJAMBURA

PILLI-PILLI

JUNGLE GREEN SALAD

FRESH PINEAPPLE WITH HONEY

CHIN-CHIN   COFFEE

The recipes for Chicken Moamba, Rice Bujambura and Jungle Green Salad are given for 8 portions and may be multiplied by 2 or 3 for the buffet.

An African Buffet   127

COLD CUCUMBER SOUP

There is nothing so refreshing as a cold cucumber soup on a hot day. This soup outsold all the others at the African Pavilion at the World's Fair in New York, 1964–65. It was not unusual to sell twenty-five gallons in one day.

Yield: 2 quarts

In a 3-quart saucepan:

Sauté	1 cup	WHITE ONIONS, chopped finely, in
	2 oz.	BUTTER.
Add	1 cup	WHITE POTATOES, peeled and in ½-inch cubes
	1 Tbs.	SALT
	¼ tsp.	WHITE PEPPER
	few drops	TABASCO
	2 quarts	CHICKEN STOCK.
Cook		until potatoes are soft and put through a seive or food mill.
Add	1 cup	SOUR CREAM and
	2 cups	CUCUMBERS, peeled and finely diced (¼-inch).
Correct the Seasoning		and chill.
Serve		in cold cups garnished with slices of cucumber with the green skin left partially on.

SHRIMP TREES

A Shrimp Tree is a fresh pineapple completely covered with cooked shrimp attached to the fruit with toothpicks. The green fronds above form a decorative top.

In a 4-quart saucepan:

Place	4 lbs.	RAW SHRIMP (15 to 20 to the pound).
Cover with		WATER from the tap.

Add	2 Tbs.	SALT
	1	LEMON cut in 8 pieces
	2	BAY LEAVES.

Bring   slowly to the boiling point. Turn off the flame.

Cool   to room temperature.

Remove   shells, black vein, and tail and wash in clean water.

Spear   each shrimp, 1 inch from the tail, with a round-ended cocktail toothpick (do not use colored toothpicks).

Place   1   FRESH PINEAPPLE on a damp dish towel.

Spear   through the shrimp into the pineapple, covering pineapple completely.

Allow   ends of toothpicks to jut out.

Form   a second layer of shrimp directly under the first. Continue until there are four rows.

Place   a damp towel around the shrimp and refrigerate the pineapple until ready to serve.

Arrange   the tree on a footed dish.

Keep   towel damp and only remove it as the buffet is about to begin.

Serve   with three pint bowls for dipping, set in front of the footed stand:

One with *Pilli-pilli* thinned to sauce texture with additional tomato paste and lemon juice.
One with regular cocktail sauce (for your less daring guests).
One with Nairobi Curry Sauce:

Stir	½ tsp.	GINGER (optional)
	1 Tbs.	CURRY POWDER and
	1 Tbs.	PAPRIKA, into
	1 pint	MAYONNAISE.

PILLI-PILLI SAUCE

Pilli-pilli is the little red hot pepper of Africa which is so important an accompaniment to the food in most of its countries. It is much like the crushed red pepper used on pizza and other continental dishes. We would find it impossible to use the quantities the Africans do—but used with discretion, it adds zing to many main dishes.

Although we have toned it down by the addition of tomato sauce, lemon juice, and onion, it is still necessary to use it with care. In the Portuguese colonies of Africa the red hot pepper is called *Piri-piri* and it is blended with lemon only.

In the Malagasy Republic it is known as *Sacha* and it is blended with oil.

Yield: 3 cups

In a 2-quart bowl:

Blend	2 cups	TOMATO SAUCE, canned
	½ cup	LEMON JUICE
	½ cup	WHITE ONIONS, very finely chopped
	1 Tbs.	GARLIC POWDER
	1 Tbs.	CRUSHED RED PEPPER (PILLI-PILLI).

Keep refrigerated in covered container.

Serve as a relish sauce in a bowl.

When used with seafood add ¼ cup grated horseradish. An excellent cocktail sauce.

Add 2 oz. (¼ cup) dry red wine for a gourmet sauce for bland meats.

Add ½ cup finely chopped fresh tomatoes as they do in some parts of Africa.

AVOCADO MOUSSE

Yield: 1 3-quart mold

In a 4-quart bowl:

Dissolve	2 packages (3¾ oz. each)	LIME-FLAVORED GELATIN and
	3 packages	LEMON-FLAVORED GELATIN in
	1 quart	BOILING WATER.
Add	3 cups	APRICOT NECTAR (or canned fruit syrup)
	1 pint	AVOCADO (mashed in blender or with fork).
Chill	until mixture becomes syrupy.	
Fold in	1 pint	SOUR CREAM.

Cut	½	AVOCADO in thin slices and arrange at bottom of 3-quart mold.
Cover		with the above mixture and chill until firm.
Dip		mold in hot water and turn out onto a 12-inch platter.
Place	¼ head	CHICORY washed and cut in small pieces around the edge.
Garnish with		FRESH FRUITS such as melon balls, strawberries, etc.

For a party of twenty-four, two molds (3 quarts each) are adequate. Prepare one avocado and one melon mold (see below) or make two of a kind.

Rhodesian Melon Mold

Yield: 1 3-quart mold

In a 4-quart bowl:

Dissolve	5 pkgs. (3¾ oz.) 1 quart	LEMON-FLAVORED GELATIN in BOILING WATER.
Add	1 quart 1 quart	ORANGE JUICE and CANTELOUPE (or any yellow ripe melon), cut in ½-inch cubes.
Chill		until mixture begins to thicken.
Stir		through for better distribution of the melon.
Pour		into a 3-quart mold and chill until set.
Whip	1 pint 4 Tbs.	HEAVY CREAM with SUGAR until stiff.
Fold in	2 oz.	CANDIED CRYSTALLIZED GINGER, chopped finely.
Dip		the mold in hot water and turn out on a 12-inch platter.
Surround	with	ROMAINE or CHICORY.
Garnish		with the whipped cream and seasonal fruits. If the mold has a hole in the center, fill it with the whipped cream.

ROAST BEEF

What is a buffet without a warm roast, sliced before you—succulent and satisfying? Ask your butcher to cut a 10 to 15-lb. round of beef (boneless) from the sirloin, one that will not require tying. The preparation is simplicity itself!

Place   ROAST BEEF in roasting pan about 12 × 18 × 2 inches.

Force   a meat thermometer (important) into the heart of the beef.

Turn   the thermometer so that you can see it when you open the oven door.

Sprinkle   GARLIC SALT and COARSE BLACK PEPPER over the roast.

Bake   at between 300° and 325°.

Allow   about 4 hours to bring the roast to 140° (rare) or 160° (medium).

Brush   the roast when nearly done with KITCHEN BOUQUET to darken.

Plan   the roast to be ready at least 1 hour before serving to give the meat a chance to "set" so that there will be a better yield and it will slice easily.

Hold   it at the back of the range, until ready to use.

Place   the roast on a cutting board when buffet is ready to begin.

Cut   against the grain with a sharp carving knife in long thin slices. Do not spear the meat with the serving fork but press the fork down on it to give you control as you slice. If ridges form you need more practice with the carving knife.

    To make the roast go further you may cut the meat in tidbit slices and place on tiny rolls or party-type (small) bread slices. Lift the bread with the meat on it with your carving knife and place on the guest's plate.

CHICKEN MOAMBA

Yield: 8 portions

In a 6-quart pot with a tight cover:

Sauté	½ cup	YELLOW ONIONS coarsely chopped in
	2 Tbs.	PEANUT OIL until soft but not brown.
Add	2 2½-lb.	CHICKENS (fryers), cut in quarters, and seasoned with salt and pepper.
Cover	tightly and simmer for 15 minutes.	
Blend	12 oz.	PEANUT BUTTER with
	1 quart	WATER.
Pour	over the chicken when smooth and cook for 10 minutes.	
Season	4	MEDIUM SWEET POTATOES, peeled and cut in half, with
	1 Tbs.	SALT and
	½ tsp.	BLACK PEPPER.
Add	to the chicken and simmer for 15 to 20 minutes or until done.	
Cook	2 lbs.	RAW SPINACH separately until spinach breaks down but is still very green (a few minutes).
Cook	1 lb.	WHITE RICE separately using package directions.
Simmer	8	EGGS very gently until hard boiled. Peel the eggs.
Arrange	½ cup	RICE on dinner plate
	1	PEELED EGG at side of rice
	1	CHICKEN PORTION
	1	SWEET-POTATO HALF
	½ cup	COOKED SPINACH
	1 to 2 Tbs.	PEANUT-BUTTER GRAVY over the chicken.
Sprinkle	1 Tbs.	CHOPPED PEANUTS over the chicken and sweet potato.
Serve	the following condiments in bowls:	
	1 pint	CHOPPED AVOCADO
	½ cup	PILLI-PILLI SAUCE
	½ cup	SHREDDED COCONUT.

RICE BUJAMBURA

This dish is really a version of Rice Pilaf, or rice cooked in chicken stock. Rice is a perennial staple which blends beautifully with flavorings and spices. When cooking rice with a stock, try to use a stock compatible with the meat dish.

Yield: 8 cups (8 to 10 portions)

In a 3-quart saucepan:

Cook	2 cups	RICE in
	5 cups	CHICKEN STOCK.
Add	4	BAY LEAVES
	1 Tbs.	SALT
	¼ tsp.	PEPPER.
Cook		until stock is absorbed and rice is done, about 20 minutes.
Add	¼ cup	CHOPPED PIMIENTO-STUFFED OLIVES.
Remove		bay leaves before serving.

Here are other ingredients which may be added to a Pilaf of Rice.
Spanish Moroccan—Rice with black olives and lemons.
Ghanaian Rice—Rice with groundnuts (peanuts).
Check Rice Liberia—Rice with spinach chopped finely.

JUNGLE GREEN SALAD

Yield: 8 portions

Combine	1 quart	FRESH SPINACH, washed, cut, thoroughly dried
	1 pint	ROMAINE, washed, cut, thoroughly dried
	1 pint	LETTUCE, washed, cut, thoroughly dried.

(See page 228 on how to prepare lettuce and greens.)

Toss		together in a 3-quart wooden bowl with Jungle Dressing below.
Arrange	½	CUCUMBER sliced thinly over top of salad (skin on).
Chop	2	HARD-BOILED EGGS coarsely and sprinkle over cucumbers.

The secret to making a good green salad is to be sure the greens are thoroughly dry so that the dressing coats the leaves and is not diluted by water. This salad makes an excellent accompaniment to a meat, fish, or poultry dinner.

Jungle Dressing

Yield: 1 quart

In a 1-quart jar:

Blend	1 pint	SALAD OIL
	1 cup	LEMON JUICE, bottled
	1 cup	COCONUT WATER from fresh coconut*
	½ cup	GRATED COCONUT
	1 Tbs.	SALT
	1 tsp.	GARLIC POWDER
	2 Tbs.	HONEY
	¼ tsp.	CURRY POWDER
	1 tsp.	FRESHLY GROUND PEPPER
	few drops	TABASCO.
Shake	well before serving.	

* If fresh coconut is not available, use the liquid from a bottle of pickles instead of coconut water. Either makes excellent French-type dressings. Or you may substitute any white French dressing to which Tabasco and a little curry powder are added.

FRESH PINEAPPLE WITH HONEY

If the pineapple is to be served from the kitchen, it is then cut into ¾-inch slices, the core removed, spread with 1 to 2 Tbs. honey per slice and 3 to 4 Tbs. moist shredded coconut sprinkled over to completely cover the pineapple. Strawberries are most attractive with this dessert but blueberries, raspberries, or blackberries can also be used effectively.

Yield: 8 servings

Trim	1	RIPE FRESH PINEAPPLE completely removing all "eyes."
Cut	down in ¾-inch lengths from top to bottom of pineapple.	
Remove	the core.	
Cut	into ¾-inch by 2-inch lengths, and place in a 2-quart bowl.	

Dribble	1 cup	HONEY over pineapple and toss to completely coat the pineapple.
Sprinkle	1 cup	SHREDDED COCONUT over the pineapple and toss again.
Garnish with	1 cup	WHOLE STRAWBERRIES with or without stems.
Arrange		compote dishes at the side of the bowl so that guests may serve themselves.

CHIN-CHIN COOKIES

Cookies are often deep-fried in Africa, and especially in the west in countries like Nigeria, Ghana, and Liberia. They have a strong spicy flavor and a most pleasing crunchiness.

Yield: 16 deep-fat-fried cookies

	In a 1-quart bowl:	
Beat	4	EGGS until light and frothy.
Add	½ cup	SUGAR and beat until smooth.
	In a 2-quart bowl:	
Place	2 cups	SELF-RISING FLOUR.
Add	2 tsp. 1 Tbs.	CINNAMON and GRATED ORANGE RIND.
Cut in	4 oz.	BUTTER or SHORTENING as for pie crust.
Blend		the egg mixture into the flour to form a dough.
Knead		lightly until smooth.
Roll		out ½ inch thick on a floured board.
Cut into		1-inch-wide shapes such as triangles, squares, rounds, etc.
Deep-Fat Fry		at 375° until golden brown and drain on a paper towel.

PART III

ADDITIONAL RECIPES

Additional Recipes

Ghana

FRUIT GIMLET

This gimlet, made with papaya only, was served us as an appetizer by Patience A. Kotei in Accra, Ghana. Subsequently, we served it using a combination of fresh fruits and it was a most delightful first course. For striking effects use champagne glasses or any attractive wine glasses for fruit cups—and chill them thoroughly.

Yield: 8 servings

Fill		8 champagne glasses with balls or squares of FRUIT from melon, watermelon, papaya, pineapple, singly or in combination (½ cup fruit per person).
Sprinkle each with	½ tsp.	CRYSTALLIZED GINGER, finely chopped.
Pour over	1 Tbs.	GIN
	1 Tbs.	LIME JUICE and
	1 tsp.	BROWN SUGAR.
Garnish with		MINT SPRIGS.
Serve		chilled on a 5- to 6-inch underliner dish.

Kenya

M'BAAZI | Pea Beans Nairobi Style

M'Baazi means "beans" in Swahili and is pronounced em-ba-ah'-zi with the voice pitched higher on the final syllable. Any kind of beans may be used except green or waxed beans. You'll be surprised to find that dried beans can taste so good! If it is not convenient to prepare the coconut milk, use 1 cup of milk and add ½ cup of finely grated packaged coconut.

Yield: 8 portions

In a 2-quart saucepan:

Simmer	1 cup	DRIED PEA BEANS in
	1 quart	BOILING SALTED WATER until tender (about one hour). Drain.

In another 2-quart saucepan:

Sauté	½ cup	ONIONS, chopped finely
	½ cup	GREEN PEPPER, chopped finely
	1 tsp.	SALT
	¼ tsp.	CRUSHED RED PEPPER in
	4 Tbs.	OIL or BUTTER until soft but not brown.

Add the drained beans and continue to sauté until the onions are brown.

Add   1 cup   COCONUT MILK (see page 225)

Simmer gently until the coconut milk thickens to medium-sauce consistency.

Correct the Seasoning

Place in 1-quart bowl and chill until thoroughly cold.

Line small sauce dishes with lettuce cups.

Dish out   ½ cup   M'BAAZI per portion.

Garnish with   1 or 2   PARSLEY SPRIGS and TOMATO WEDGES.

United Arab Republic

FOOL MUDAMMAS | Egyptian Lentils

To make authentic *Fool Mudammas* try to buy the pink-colored Egyptian lentils available in gourmet and specialty shops. These tiny beans are a versatile staple. They make an interesting addition to soups or can be served alone as a starchy vegetable.

Yield: 8 servings

In a 2-quart bowl:

Soak	1 cup	EGYPTIAN LENTILS or WHITE BEANS overnight, in water to cover.
Drain and Cover with	3 cups	WATER in a 1-quart saucepan.
Add	1 Tbs.	SALT.
Cook		until the skins split—about 1 hour.
Drain and Chill		
Add	½ tsp.	SALT
	2 cloves	GARLIC, mashed or finely minced
	½ cup	OLIVE OIL
	¼ cup	LEMON JUICE and blend.
Chill		
Arrange	cups of	ROMAINE or other loose head lettuce on salad plates.
Place	¼ cup (4 Tbs.)	ABOVE MIXTURE in a mound on each lettuce cup.
Garnish each with	2 or 3	SCALLIONS, trimmed to 3-inch lengths.

South Africa

YELLOW MELON MUSCADEL

Muscadel is the South African name for our Muscatel. Wines are used extensively in the preparation of fruit appetizers.

Yield: 8 servings, ½ melon each

	About 3 hours before serving:	
Prepare	following syrup:	
Boil together for 5 minutes	1 cup	SUGAR
	1½ cups	WATER or FRUIT JUICE
	2 Tbs.	LEMON JUICE
	2 Tbs.	VINEGAR
	1 tsp.	GROUND GINGER.
Strain	through a cheesecloth and cool.	
Serrate	4 small	CANTELOUPES (or any small melons) zigzagging across center with a knife to give uniform halves.
Remove seeds		
Sprinkle	salt and pepper.	
Pour	2 Tbs.	SWEET WINE (a MUSCATEL or PORT) in each melon half.
Fill each with	¼ cup	WATERMELON BALLS.
Pour	about 2 to 3 Tbs. syrup over each melon.	
Refrigerate	for several hours before serving.	
Garnish with	1 or 2 sprigs	MINT.
Serve	on salad plates.	

South Africa

Here is another melon idea: Cut a 2-inch circular plug out of a cantaloupe—scoop out seeds and fibers. Fill melon with diced fresh pineapple and strawberries, add 3 Tbs. port wine or any sweet brandy. Replace top and seal it by spreading cold butter on the seam. Chill. Cut in half to serve.

Malagasy

AVOCADO DIP

Yield: 1 quart

In a 2-quart bowl:

Peel 4   AVOCADO PEARS (soft), cut in small pieces, and mash smooth.

Add 4 Tbs.   LEMON JUICE and blend with the mashed avocados.

Add 2 1¼-oz.
cans   ANCHOVY FILLETS, cut in ½-inch pieces
½ cup   SWEET WHITE ONIONS (Spanish), chopped finely
1 tsp.   CRUSHED RED PEPPERS
½ tsp.   GARLIC POWDER.

Mix in a blender or chop finely.

Add ½ cup   SWEET SHERRY.

Cover the bowl with aluminum foil and chill until ready to use.

Serve with sesame crackers.

To serve the dip as an appetizer, arrange individual lettuce cups on salad plates, place the dip in the lettuce cups and garnish with thin onion slices and tomato wedges. You may serve this with sesame crackers.

To serve the dip as a snack, place the dip in a glass bowl garnished with parsley surrounded by crackers on a platter.

Senegal

L'ASSIETTE DES ASSIETTES | White Fish on Black-eyed Peas

> *L'Assiette des Assiettes* means "the dish of dishes." In Senegal the term is used to refer to the appetizer of appetizers, white fish on black-eyed peas, a dish featured in every good restaurant in Dakar. Only the sauce varies. The one above was given to us by M. Mamadou of Les Cannibales Deux. (The heart of palm may be purchased in a gourmet shop or omitted if desired.)

Yield: Individual portion

On a dinner plate:

Arrange	1	BED OF LETTUCE.
Place	3 Tbs.	COOKED BLACK-EYED PEAS in center of plate.
Place	a 3-inch square piece	COOKED FISH (haddock or halibut) on the peas.
Surround with	2	TOMATO SLICES overlapping
	3	CUCUMBER SLICES
	1 or 2	PIECES HEART OF PALM
	½	HARD-BOILED EGG.
Mask	the fish with the following dressing (enough for 8 portions):	
Combine	1 bottle	TOMATO CATSUP
	1 tsp.	WORCESTERSHIRE SAUCE
	½ cup	WHITE VINEGAR
	3 Tbs.	SUGAR
	½ cup	ONION, chopped finely.
Chill	thoroughly before serving.	

Ghana

LIGHT SOUP | Chicken Vegetable Soup

In Africa, there are light soups and there are dark soups. Light soups are made with meat, fish, or poultry for the basic stock. The soups are thickened with white beans or else with melon seeds which are prepared in the same manner but are ground to a paste called *Egusi.* Dark soups are made with groundnuts (peanuts) which are mashed to a pulp before they are added to the stock.

Yield: 8 to 12 portions

In a 4-quart kettle:

Place
1 3-lb.	CHICKEN, whole
1 cup	WHITE PEA BEANS
1 cup	ONIONS, chopped coarsely
½ cup	GREEN PEPPER, chopped coarsely
2 quarts	WATER
1 Tbs.	SALT
½ tsp.	PEPPER
½ tsp.	CRUSHED RED PEPPER (optional).

Bring up to boil and simmer until chicken is done.

Remove the chicken and put aside for use in an entrée later.

Add
1 16-oz. can	WHOLE TOMATOES (crush them first—2 cups)
2 cups	EGGPLANT, cut in 1-inch cubes
1 16-oz. can	OKRA (optional).

Simmer until beans are thoroughly cooked and soup has reduced by one-quarter.

Correct the Seasoning to your taste.

HOT AVOCADO SOUP

The subtle pale green color and semisoft texture of avocados make them one of the most exotic of foods. Shrimp, crabmeat, and lobster are more delicious than ever when combined with avocado. For avocado lovers we have included avocado hot in soups, cold in soups, in a mousse, stuffed, and in desserts.

Yield: 8 servings

In a 3-quart saucepan:

Place 6 cups   CHICKEN BROTH.

Add   2 2-oz.
           pkgs.   WHITE SAUCE MIX (prepare as directed on package).

Cook   over medium heat until broth thickens to cream soup consistency.

Add   2   AVOCADOS mashed to a pulp and
           ¼ cup   WHITE ONION (Spanish) grated.

Bring to the boiling point and serve each cup piping hot with

           1 Tbs.   SOUR CREAM (or whipped cream) as a garnish and
           1 slice   AVOCADO topping the cream.

ICED AVOCADO SOUP

Yield: 8 soup cups

In an electric blender:

Combine 2 8-oz.
             cans   CREAM VICHYSSOISE, frozen (thawed)
             2 cups   MILK
             2   AVOCADOS, in pieces.

Beat   at high speed until thoroughly blended.

Chill

Serve   in cups topped with sour cream and chives.

South Africa

ROCK LOBSTER SOUP

Rock Lobster Soup is, of course, the king of soups. It is for special occasions and when you need an outstanding dish to start your menu. You may also follow the same recipe using crabmeat or our own Maine lobster.

Yield: 8 servings

In a 2-quart saucepan:

Simmer	1 lb.	ROCK LOBSTER TAILS in
until	1½ quarts	WATER and
tender	1 tsp.	SALT. Reserve water.

In a 3-quart saucepan:

Sauté	1 cup	ONIONS, thinly sliced in
	4 oz.	BUTTER until soft but not brown.
Add	2 medium	TOMATOES, cut into small wedges
	1 clove	GARLIC, mashed
	1 tsp.	SALAD HERBS
	½ tsp.	NUTMEG
	1 tsp.	SALT
	½ tsp.	PEPPER and
	1 piece	LEMON PEEL.

Simmer for 15 minutes.

Add 1 cup   DRY WHITE WINE

Heat until it bubbles.

Add 1 quart   WATER from Rock Lobster.

Cook for 5 minutes longer.

Put mixture through food mill or sieve.

Add the lobster meat chopped finely and
½ cup   LIGHT CREAM.

Correct the Seasoning

Serve in soup cups.

West Africa

CHILLED PAWPAW SOUP

Papaya is the fruit of the pawpaw tree. Papaya nectar is available in the better grocery stores and is the base for the Pawpaw Soup. Use fresh papayas when they are available. If papaya nectar is not available, use apricot nectar. Slices of yellow melon may be substituted if desired.

Chicken stock may be prepared from a packaged or canned chicken soup but is best when made from scratch as in Groundnut Soup (see page 109.

Yield: 2 quarts

Blend	1 quart	CHICKEN STOCK
	1 pint	SOUR CREAM
	1 12-oz. can	PAPAYA NECTAR
	½ cup	FRESH PAPAYA or YELLOW MELON finely chopped.
Add	1 Tbs. each	LEMON JUICE and RIND
	1 tsp.	SALT.
Chill	thoroughly.	
Garnish	with slices of papaya or yellow melon.	
Serve	in soup cups.	

South Africa

MEALIE SOUP SUPERB | Super Corn Soup   **Yield:** 8 servings

In a 4-quart saucepan:

Sauté	1 cup	YELLOW ONIONS, finely chopped, in
	2 oz.	BUTTER until soft but not brown.
Add	1 cup	FRESH TOMATOES, cut in ½-inch pieces.
Simmer	for about 3 minutes.	
Add	2 cups	CANNED KERNEL CORN
	2 cups	CREAM-STYLE CANNED CORN
	1 can	EVAPORATED MILK

3 cups	CHICKEN STOCK (or use water and 3 chicken-bouillon cubes)
1 Tbs.	SALT
1 tsp.	COARSE BLACK PEPPER.

Simmer   gently covered for 15 minutes.

Serve   piping hot with crackers.

One of the secrets in making a good corn soup or chowder with a creamy texture is evaporated milk. The next time you make a New England style clam or fish chowder, try evaporated milk instead of cream or milk.

Tanzania

M'TORI SUPU | Cream of Banana Soup

This soup should be the consistency of heavy cream. If fresh coconut is used, add the coconut water as part of the liquid, grate coconut, and prepare coconut milk as directed on page 226, after mixture has been puréed. This soup may also be made with chicken, in which case a 5- to 6-lb. fowl is used and cooked whole.

Yield: 8 servings

In a 4-quart saucepan:

Simmer
2 lbs.	STEWING BEEF with bone, in one piece
½ cup	ONIONS, chopped coarsely
1 tsp.	SALT
½ tsp.	PEPPER
¼ tsp.	CRUSHED RED PEPPER in
2 quarts	WATER for about 1 hour.

Add
3 medium	POTATOES, peeled and cut in chunks
4 medium	BANANAS, peeled and cut in chunks

Simmer   until meat is completely tender.

Remove   meat and set aside.

Put   mixture through a food mill or sieve.

Add
2 oz.	BUTTER and
1 cup	COCONUT MILK (see page 226).

Serve   meat separately, as an entrée.

Somali

SOMALI CRABMEAT STEW

If scallop shells are available, spoon mixture into shells, piling them high and serve with rice. This makes a very elegant dish.

Yield: 8 portions

In a 3-quart heavy saucepan:

Sauté	1 cup	ONIONS, finely chopped
	1 tsp.	CURRY POWDER
	1 tsp.	GINGER
	1 tsp.	SALT
	1 tsp.	CRUSHED RED PEPPER in
	¼ cup	PEANUT OIL or BUTTER until onions are soft but not brown.
Add	1 lb.	TOMATOES cut in small wedges.
Simmer	until tomatoes begin to cook.	
Add	2 lbs.	CRABMEAT (or any seafood).
Sauté	lightly for 10 minutes.	
Serve	crabmeat over hot rice (2 cups rice to 5 cups water).	

Ethiopia

BROILED FISH | *From Chef Kurt Linsi*

Chef Kurt Linsi of the Ethiopian Airlines was chef for Emperor Haile Selassie for ten years. He is one of the world's outstanding cooks. We love his method of broiling fish.

Place	2 or 3 freshly caught WHOLE FISH, cleaned, on a wire rack.
Lower	the rack carefully into a long pan of salted lukewarm water.
Bring	the water up to a boil slowly and simmer until the skin loosens.
Lift	the fish out *rack and all* and place it directly over a hot charcoal fire.

Sprinkle with salt and pepper and, as soon as the fish begins to flake, remove from fire and serve immediately.

If fish appears dry brush it carefully with seasoned oil or butter (see page 227).

South Africa

FISH PIE

This is a great favorite in South Africa and a good luncheon to make on a busy day as it is simple to prepare. It can also be made with leftover meat or chicken. If you want to save time, you can use instant mashed potatoes and add to them a little onion sautéed in oil (not butter) to improve their flavor.

Yield: 8 servings

In a 2-quart saucepan:

Sauté	1 cup	ONIONS, chopped
	½ tsp.	PEPPER
	2 tsp.	SALT
	½ tsp.	DRY MUSTARD in
	2 oz.	BUTTER or MARGARINE.
Add	3 cups	COLD STEAMED FISH, cleaned from bones and flaked.
Add	1 8-oz. can	TOMATO SAUCE
	½ cup	MASHED POTATOES and
	1	EGG, beaten lightly.
Pack	in a buttered 10-inch deep pie dish.	
Spread	2 cups	MASHED POTATOES over top.
Brush with	1	EGG, beaten, and thinned with
	2 Tbs.	WATER.
Bake	at 350° for 30 minutes or until golden brown on top.	
Cut	pie in 8 wedges and serve.	

Tanzania

SAMAKI WA KUKUANGO | Steamed Whole Fish with Sautéed Onions

> We discovered this marvelous fish in an out-of-the-way restaurant in Dar Es Salaam. It was superb. The cook had prepared extra sautéed onions with tomatoes and held them aside as additional garnish. This might be a good idea for you.

Yield: 8 to 10 portions

Scale and clean	1 4- to 6-lb. WHOLE FISH (like red snapper, haddock, halibut, etc.)— one that will fit into a roasting pan.
Remove	head if desired and cut gashes 2 inches apart across the entire fish.

In a small bowl:

Combine	2 Tbs.	SALT
	1 tsp.	GARLIC POWDER (or use fresh garlic crushed)
	1 tsp.	COARSE RED PEPPER.

Rub	the seasoned salt into the gashes thoroughly. Allow to stand for 15 minutes.

In a 7-inch skillet:

Sauté	1 cup	ONIONS, chopped coarsely or sliced, and
	1 cup	TOMATOES, sliced, in
	2 Tbs.	BUTTER, with a lid on the pan.

Place	the fish on a rack in a roasting pan.
Fill	bottom of pan with water up to the rack.
Spread	the onion mixture all over the fish.
Simmer	or bake at 350° for 30 to 40 minutes or until fish is done.
Remove	the lid and permit the water to evaporate or reduce by one-quarter.
Remove	the fish carefully to a large platter.
Spread	the onion mixture over the top of the fish as a garnish.
Serve	with rice at the side, with the fish sauce, and with lemon slices.

East Africa

SHRIMP CURRY

Any size shrimp may be used in this curried dish, but small shrimp (over twenty-five per pound) are just as satisfactory and far less expensive than the large shrimp.

Yield: 8 portions

In a 4-quart saucepan:

Sauté	1 cup	CHOPPED ONION
	1 tsp.	GARLIC POWDER
	1 Tbs.	CURRY POWDER
	1 tsp.	TURMERIC
	1 Tbs.	SALT
	½ tsp.	CHILI POWDER in
	2 oz.	BUTTER or OIL until soft but not brown.
Add	1 cup	COCONUT CREAM (see page 226)
	2 lbs.	SHRIMP, uncooked and peeled
	2 cups	POTATOES, diced, and
	1 cup	WATER.
Simmer		until tender, about 20 minutes, covered tightly.
Add	2 oz.	LEMON JUICE
	1 cup	COCONUT CREAM.
Cook		until slightly thickened—about 10 minutes more.*
Serve		hot with rice and accompaniments such as the following in a large sectioned relish dish:

       FRIED ONION RINGS
       CHOPPED BANANAS
       CHOPPED CUCUMBERS
       RAISINS
       MANGO OR PINEAPPLE CHUTNEY
       SHREDDED COCONUT—toasted or plain (see page 225).

* If a thicker curry is desired, dissolve 2 Tbs. cornstarch in 2 Tbs. water and add in the last few minutes of cooking.

Liberia

FRESH FISH IN COCONUT CREAM WITH FOO-FOO (FU-FU)

Yield: 8 portions

Prepare	3 cups	COCONUT CREAM (see page 226).

In a 12-inch skillet (electric if possible):

Sauté	1 lb.	ONIONS, thinly sliced
	1 tsp.	SALT
	½ tsp.	BLACK PEPPER
	1 tsp.	CRUSHED RED PEPPER or few drops TABASCO in
	4 oz.	BUTTER until soft but not brown.
Cut in halves	4 1-lb	WHOLE FRESH FISH (trout, sea bass, pike, etc.), cleaned, with heads removed.

Season with salt and pepper.

Sauté fish in the butter mixture for 1 minute on each side.

Pour the coconut milk over the fish.

Cover tightly and simmer gently for 10 minutes.

Remove cover and baste constantly until fish is done and sauce has thickened to a cream consistency (about 10 minutes).

Lay fish out on a platter with a spatula and pour the sauce over it.

Serve with *Foo-Foo (Fu-Fu).*

FOO-FOO (or FU-FU) | Cassava or Yam

Foo-Foo is pounded cassava or yam. It can be made from any mashed starchy vegetable and used as an accompaniment for a meat or fish entree.

Yield: 8 portions

Cook	3 lbs.	POTATOES in boiling salted water. Use either sweet potatoes, white potatoes, or yams, or a combination of any of them.

Remove	the skins and mash.	
Season	to taste. Butter may be added but do not add liquid.	

A quick *Foo-Foo* can be made with instant mashed potatoes. Cut down on the amount of liquid required in the directions to give a heavy consistency.

South Africa

CAPE KEDGEREE | Fish and Rice

Kedgeree, a rice and fish combination which originated in India, originally was made with curry. The dish was adopted by the English and the curry was eliminated. If you like the flavor of curry, cook it with the rice (about 1 tsp. per cup of rice), as it adds an interesting flavor. In India fish and rice are usually prepared in equal amounts. In South Africa twice as much fish as rice is used.

Yield: 8 servings

In a 2-quart saucepan:

Melt	2 oz.	BUTTER or MARGARINE.
Add	4 cups	COOKED FISH, flaked, and stir gently.
Add	2 cups	COOKED RICE and
	4	EGG WHITES, hard-boiled, chopped coarsely
	2 tsp.	SALT
	½ tsp.	PEPPER
	½ cup	EVAPORATED MILK or LIGHT CREAM.
Stir	gently over the fire until thoroughly hot.	
Garnish the mixture with	4	EGG YOLKS, passed through a fine wire sieve.

Zanzibar

MASALE | Fried Fish

Africans have an interesting method of preserving their fish by frying. You might try this if you made a large catch of fish or your neighbor brought some of his lucky catch to you.

Clean and Scale	whole fish and remove insides.	
Cut	3 large deep diagonal gashes on each side.	
Combine	1 Tbs.	COARSE SALT
	¼ tsp.	GARLIC POWDER
	¼ tsp.	COARSE RED PEPPER, ground, for each fish.
Rub	salt mixture well into gashes on both sides.	
Fry in	1 cup	HOT OIL until light brown.
Reduce	heat and continue frying slowly until fish is quite brown but not burned.	
Lift	fish from fat. Wrap in brown paper while still hot, cool, and refrigerate. The fish will stay fresh for two weeks or longer if refrigerated.	

South Africa

BAKED LOBSTER TAIL SOUFFLÉ

Lobster tails are expensive and this is a good recipe for making them go a long way.

Yield: 8 portions

Preparation of lobster:

Cover	8 6-oz.	AFRICAN ROCK LOBSTER TAILS with warm water from tap.
Add	1 Tbs.	SALT and
	½	LEMON cut in wedges. Cover.
Simmer	slowly for 5 minutes.	

Turn	off the flame.	
Allow	to stand in the water for 30 minutes.	
Cool	and drain.	
Split	the soft (under) side of the tail around the edges and remove the meat.
Cut	the meat into 8 uniform pieces and place in a 1-gallon bowl.

Blend in	2 cups	HONEYDEW MELON, peeled and cut in ¾-inch squares
	½ cup	BREAD CRUMBS
	½ cup	WHITE SAUCE (from a mix)
	1 Tbs.	CURRY POWDER
	1 Tbs.	PAPRIKA.

| **Fold in** | 5 | EGG WHITES beaten stiff. |

| **Stuff** | the lobster tails with this mixture, piling it as high as possible and rounding it out with a spatula. |

| **Arrange** | the tails on a cookie sheet and bake at 425° for about 10 minutes until golden brown. |

| **Serve with** | RICE BUJAMBURA (page 133). |

Ghana

SMOKED FISH STEW

Smoked fish is used in many combination dishes in West Africa but rarely by itself in a stew. We discovered this excellent stew in—of all places— the Y.W.C.A. in Accra, Ghana. A tiny young girl made the stew in a huge pot for about one hundred lunch guests, including ourselves. It was delicious!

We made this stew in our test kitchen in New York using smoked white-fish, and the dish evoked much enthusiastic response.

Yield: 2 quarts (8 portions)

In a 4-quart saucepan:

| **Sauté** | ½ lb. | ONIONS, thinly sliced in |

	¼ cup	VEGETABLE OIL until soft but not brown.
Add	1 lb.	FRESH TOMATOES cut in 1-inch pieces.
	4 Tbs.	TOMATO PASTE
	½ tsp.	CRUSHED RED PEPPER (optional)
	1 quart	WATER.

Simmer with cover on for 15 minutes.

Debone 2 lbs. SMOKED FISH (if smoked herring is used, soak it for 1 hour to remove excess salt).

Add the deboned, flaked fish and simmer for 10 minutes longer.

Correct the Seasoning with salt (if needed) and pepper.

Add water if necessary to bring to stew consistency.

Serve with RICE.

Tanzania

DAGAA | Dried Fish Sautéed with Tomatoes

Be sure to check the saltiness of the dried codfish. It may need to be soaked overnight. If codfish tends to stick to pan in sauting, add 1 to 2 oz. butter but avoid stirring. Browning the fish is the secret of the flavor of the dish. If the fish is still too salty, soak it in cold water after browning.

In our country we tend to use codfish only in making codfish cakes. In Africa, dried fish is used often and in many different ways. It is interesting to note that most African dried fish come from Scandinavia and Iceland.

Yield: 8 portions

In a 10-inch Teflon skillet or pot:

Sauté without oil 2 lbs. DRIED CODFISH cut in 2-inch chunks until slightly brown.

In a 4-quart saucepan:

Bring to a boil	1 lb.	TOMATOES, cut in small wedges
	1 cup	ONIONS, chopped coarsely
	1 small	CHILI PEPPER, cut in small pieces (optional)

	2 cloves	GARLIC, minced finely
	1 pint	WATER
	1 pint	COCONUT MILK (see page 226).

Add the sautéed codfish (desalted).

Simmer gently until most of the water is absorbed. Stir carefully to avoid breaking up fish.

Add 2 oz.   BUTTER and allow it to melt over the DAGAA.

Serve with   MASHED BANANAS and UGALI or RICE.

Nigeria

NIGERIAN PANCAKES WITH SHRIMP

The pancakes are a meal in themselves, and require no other accompaniment than a green salad.

Yield: 16 medium pancakes

In a quart bowl:

Soak 1 lb.   PEA BEANS (any white beans will do) in water to cover overnight.

Drain excess water, and then in a 1-quart saucepan cover again with fresh water and

Add 1 Tbs.   SALT.

Simmer slowly until tender.

Drain and put through a food mill or sieve into a 3-quart bowl.

Add
½ lb.	FRESH TOMATOES, cut in ¼-inch cubes.
½ lb.	YELLOW ONIONS, finely chopped
1 lb.	COOKED SHRIMP, in ½-inch pieces
1 Tbs.	SALT
¼ tsp.	BLACK PEPPER
¼ tsp.	CAYENNE PEPPER
6 large	EGGS, beaten lightly.

In a large skillet:

Heat ½ cup   PEANUT or any VEGETABLE OIL.

Drop the mixture by heaping tablespoons in the hot fat. It will spread out like a pancake.

Turn when the bottom is brown and firm.

Serve 2 pancakes as a portion.

Ivory Coast

HALIBUT IVORY COAST

Africans prepare fish in many interesting ways. Coconut is often used in cooking fish, as are pumpkin and squash as presented in the recipe below. In this dish the rice absorbs the flavors of all the ingredients and seasonings in the steaming process with most delicious results. This is an ideal dish to cook in individual casseroles if you have them. The secret is to cover the casseroles tightly so that the rice steams. Use aluminum foil if your casseroles do not have lids.

Yield: 8 portions

In a 6-quart Dutch oven or casserole baking dish:

Sauté 2 cups   YELLOW ONIONS chopped finely with
1 tsp.   CRUSHED RED PEPPER
1 Tbs.   SALT
1 tsp.   BLACK PEPPER in
4 oz.   PEANUT OIL until soft but not brown.

Peel 2 lbs.   PUMPKIN (or yellow squash). Cut in 1-inch slices and lay over the onions.

Place 2½ lbs. HALIBUT filleted, cut in ½- to ¾-inch slices, carefully over the pumpkin.

Arrange 1 cup   COCONUT peeled and cut in 1-inch strips over the fish.

Pour 2 cups   WHITE RICE, uncooked, over the coconut and sprinkle with salt.

Combine	2 quarts	WATER with the
		WATER from the COCONUT and
	1 6-oz. can	TOMATO PASTE.
Pour		this liquid into the pot carefully so as not to disturb contents.
Cover		tightly and allow to cook gently for about 30 minutes or until rice, fish, and vegetables are tender and the liquid is absorbed.
Serve		directly from the dish in which it is cooked. Do *not* stir before serving.
Section		out portions, cut through, and remove with a wide spatula.

Senegal

THEBOUIDIENNE | Fish in the Manner of Dakar

Any fish goes well in a *Thebouidienne* (pronounced CHEB-O-DJIN). If you use fillet of sole or flounder, roll up the fillets before cooking in this manner. We found this recipe in an out-of-the-way restaurant in Dakar frequented only by the Senegalese and consider it one of the best dishes in Africa.

Yield: 8 portions

In a 6-quart Dutch oven:

Sauté	1 cup	ONIONS, chopped finely
	½ cup	GREEN PEPPERS, chopped
	1 tsp.	SALT
	¼ tsp.	CAYENNE PEPPER in
	4 oz.	OIL or MARGARINE until lightly browned.
Add	1 6-oz. can	TOMATO PASTE and
	3 6-oz. cans	WATER. Blend smooth.
Lay	8 ½-lb. pieces	FISH FILLET such as haddock, halibut, etc., at bottom of pan.
Lay over fish	8 wedges	CABBAGE, 2 inches wide
	8 halves	SWEET POTATO.

Cover		tightly and simmer for one hour over low heat until vegetables and fish are done.
Add	1 4-oz. jar	WHOLE PIMIENTOS and cook for 2 minutes longer.

In a large soup plate:

Arrange	1 cup	COOKED RICE as a bed.
Place	1	FISH PORTION in the center.
Arrange around the fish	1 1 1 1	CABBAGE WEDGE SWEET POTATO HALF WHOLE PIMIENTO HOT CHILI PEPPER (from a jar).

Guinea

AFRICAN GUINEA HENS

Try this recipe with Rock Cornish game hens. They are most compatible with the sweet potatoes and bananas. If game hens are not available use chicken. This is a great dish. Don't forget to serve *Pilli-pilli* as a side dish.

Yield: 8 half hens

In a 6-quart heavy pan:

Sauté	½ cup 2 cloves ½ lb.	ONIONS chopped coarsely GARLIC, minced, in BUTTER or OIL.
Sprinkle	4 2½-lb.	GUINEA HENS or any game hens cut in 8 to 12 pieces each with SALT, CAYENNE PEPPER, and PAPRIKA.
Sauté		on all sides until golden brown.
Add	2 cups 2 3	CHICKEN STOCK or WATER BAY LEAVES TOMATOES, cut in tiny wedges

| 4 large | SWEET POTATOES, peeled and cut in 1-inch chunks |
| 4 | FIRM BANANAS, peeled and cut in 1-inch chunks (plantains may be used if available). |

Correct the Seasonings   It may need a few drops of Tabasco.

Cook   2 cups   WHITE RICE in
4 to 5 cups   BOILING SALTED WATER until tender.

Serve   the African fowl over the rice.

Mozambique

FRANGO A PORTUGUESA | Chicken the Portuguese Way

The addition of wine is what makes this dish characteristically Portuguese. In a Mozambique kitchen, a handful of red-hot peppers would be added to the pot. We have added just a little *Piri-piri* (hot red pepper) to make it spicy enough to resemble the African dish but still cool enough for our American palates.

Yield: 8 portions

In an electric skillet (or large sauté pan):

Brown   3 2½-lb.   CHICKENS, cut up in small pieces and
seasoned with salt and pepper, in
4 to 6 oz.   BUTTER, on all sides.

Remove   pieces of chicken as they brown.

Add   1 cup   ONION, chopped finely and
1 clove   GARLIC, minced finely and cook until onions soften.

Blend in   2 Tbs.   FLOUR.

Add   2 cups   CANNED WHOLE TOMATOES, broken up by hand
¼ cup   SHERRY
1 Tbs.   SALT
1 tsp.   CRUSHED RED PEPPER.

Simmer   covered for 45 minutes.

Serve   over rice (in Portugal mashed potatoes take the place of rice).

South Africa

HOENDER PASTEI | Boer Chicken Pie

Yield: 8 portions

In a 4-quart saucepan:

Simmer
1 5- to 6-lb.	FOWL (hen)
1½ quarts	WATER
½ tsp.	MIXED PICKLING SPICES
1 Tbs.	SALT
2 medium	ONIONS, peeled, whole
4	CARROTS, peeled, whole
	until fowl is tender.

Strain the broth.

Cut fowl away from bones and skin, leaving meat in large chunks.

Slice the carrots.

In a 2-quart saucepan:

Melt 2 oz.   BUTTER

Add 6 Tbs.   FLOUR and cook until roux thickens.

Add
3 cups	CHICKEN BROTH
¼ cup	WHITE WINE
½ tsp. each	SALT and PEPPER.

Stir until medium sauce consistency.

Beat
2	EGG YOLKS with
4 Tbs.	LEMON JUICE until frothy.

Beat a little sauce into the eggs and then add mixture to pan.

Cook slowly until sauce thickens a little more.

In a 4-quart deep dish (oblong or round):

Lay out the meat uniformly at bottom of pie dish.

Arrange
3	HARD-BOILED EGGS in slices over the meat and
4 oz.	DANISH HAM sliced thinly and cut in thirds over eggs.

Spread the sliced carrots over the ham.

Cover with the sauce.

Roll out	1 package	PIE CRUST, prepared according to package directions, 1 inch larger than size of dish.
Fold		in half and lay it over the pie, then gradually unfold it so that it covers entire dish.
Press		along the edge firmly and trim excess. Score in several places to allow steam to escape.
Brush with	1 1 Tbs.	EGG thinned with WATER.
Bake		at 450° for 10 minutes and reduce heat to 375° for 30 minutes longer until golden brown.

Congo

CONGOLESE CHICKEN WITH PEANUTS

Prepare the green peppers while the chicken is baking. In the Congo the green peppers are actually burned in the fire until they are quite black and then cooked with the chicken.

Yield: 8 portions

Cut	4 2½-lb.	CHICKENS in quarters.
Brush with	4 Tbs.	MELTED BUTTER and
Sprinkle with		SALT.
Arrange		chicken quarters on a baking sheet breast side down.
Bake		at 350° for 30 minutes and turn them over breast side up.
Blend	½ cup ¼ cup	PEANUT BUTTER with MAYONNAISE.
Brush		peanut-butter mixture over the chickens to cover completely.
Bake		for 15 minutes longer until chicken is done.
Remove		from oven.

Sprinkle	½ cup	CHOPPED PEANUTS uniformly over the chicken.
Blanch	3	GREEN PEPPERS in boiling water until the skins loosen.
Remove		skins and seeds and cut peppers into 1-inch strips.
Sauté		the peppers in just enough VEGETABLE OIL to keep them from burning, and until quite dark brown.
Sprinkle		the sautéed peppers around the chicken upon serving.
Serve		with yellow rice on a large platter or with Rice Bujambura (page 133).

West Africa

GROUNDNUT STUFFING FOR ROAST CHICKEN

Yield: stuffing for 1 6-lb. chicken

In a 1-pint saucepan:

Cook the Giblets of	1 6-lb.	ROASTING CHICKEN in water to cover.

In a 2-quart bowl:

Combine	2 cups	COOKED SWEET POTATOES or YAMS, mashed
	¼ cup	ONION, chopped finely
	1	TOMATO, peeled and chopped finely
	¼ cup	PEANUTS, chopped coarsely
	2	EGGS
	1 clove	GARLIC, mashed
	1 tsp.	SALT
	¼ tsp.	THYME
		THE COOKED GIBLETS, chopped finely
	few drops	TABASCO.
Blend in	2 oz.	MELTED BUTTER.
Clean		chicken and wipe thoroughly dry.
Stuff		bird with above mixture. Also stuff the neck.
Criss-Cross		the legs of chicken in front of opening and tie with a clean cord.

Fold   skin of neck around back of chicken and skewer down with a strong tooth-pick.

Force   wings around back (this will also hold down skin of neck).

Spread   with softened SEASONED BUTTER (see page 227) uniformly on all parts of skin.

Place   on a baking pan *breast side down,* using a "V" rack (purchased in a department store).

Roast   at 325° for 30 minutes.

Turn Bird   and continue to roast breast side up for 30 minutes.

Brush   from time to time with more softened butter if required.

You may like the brown-bag method of roasting chicken. If so, place chicken in a brown paper bag after brushing with seasoned butter. Roast breast side down at 300° for 1 hour. Tear away bag, turn, and permit chicken to brown to desired color, breast side up.

Nigeria

CHICKEN AND BEEF LOAF, NIGERIAN STYLE

This Nigerian recipe is an ideal way to use leftover beef and chicken. Together they make a most appetizing combination. Keep the cold loaf for sandwiches and hors d'oeuvres, etc. It is wonderful for picnics as this loaf is good hot or cold.

Yield: 8 4-oz. portions

In a 2-quart bowl:

Combine   leftover chicken and beef to make 2 lbs. (4 cups firmly packed).

Chop   finely or put through a meat grinder.

Add   1 tsp.   SALT
         1 tsp.   GROUND GINGER
         ¼ tsp.   CAYENNE PEPPER

½ cup	ONION, chopped
½ cup	BREAD CRUMBS
1 tsp.	SALT
few drops	TABASCO
4	EGGS, beaten.

Correct the Seasoning

Pack   into a well-greased 2-lb. loaf pan.

Bake   at 350° for 1 hour.

Unmold   and cut in slices.

Use   as a meat loaf and serve with your favorite TOMATO SAUCE or CHICKEN GRAVY.

Liberia

PEARLU RICE | Chicken and Ham in a Stew

Pearlu Rice is one of the most popular dishes in Liberia. It is a "dinner in a dish" entrée and all that is required with it is a green salad such as our Jungle Salad (see page 133).

Serve Pearlu Rice in a large bowl, and allow everyone to help themselves.

Yield: 8 portions

Cut   1 3-lb.   CHICKEN in 8 serving pieces.

Wash,   drain, and dry. Spread out and allow to stand for 15 minutes.

Dip   in flour seasoned with SALT, PEPPER, AND PAPRIKA.

In a 9-inch heavy skillet:

Brown chicken in   1 cup   COOKING OIL, on all sides.

Transfer   to a 6-quart Dutch oven or heavy pot.

Brown   2 lbs.   HAM (oven ready) cut in 1-inch cubes on all sides, in the same skillet.

Add   to the pot:

½ cup	ONIONS chopped coarsely
2 cups	CABBAGE chopped coarsely.

Blend

2 quarts	WATER
1 6-oz. can	TOMATO PASTE
1 Tbs.	SALT
½ tsp.	BLACK PEPPER
few drops	TABASCO.

Add   the liquid to the pot.

Simmer   covered for 30 minutes.

Remove   chicken from the pot.

Add   2½ cups   BROWN RICE (uncooked).

Cook   for 45 minutes, adding water if necessary during cooking.

Return   chicken to pot about 5 minutes before ready to serve.

Nigeria

CHICKEN IMOYO | Chicken and Okra

Imoyo refers to the name given dishes of this type by slaves liberated from Brazil who settled in Lagos. Very often onions, peppers, and tomatoes are not cooked but added raw at the last moment. *Imoyo* is generally served with cassava flour dumplings cooked in the drained chicken stock.

Yield: 8 portions

In a 4-quart saucepan:

Place

2 3-lb.	CHICKENS cut in serving pieces.
2 tsp.	SALT
¼ tsp.	PEPPER
¼ tsp.	CRUSHED RED PEPPER
2 medium	ONIONS, peeled and cut in quarters.
2 quarts	WATER.

Simmer   gently for 30 minutes.

Add	4	TOMATOES, cut in halves.
	1 lb.	FRESH OKRA, ends cut and left whole
		(if not available use 1 16-oz. can okra drained, but add it during the last 5 minutes of cooking).
	4	GREEN BELL PEPPERS, cleaned and cut in quarters
	1 tsp.	CHILI POWDER (optional) or use ½ tsp. crushed red pepper
	4 Tbs.	TOMATO PURÉE or PASTE
	2 Tbs.	LEMON or LIME JUICE.

Simmer until vegetables and chicken are cooked.

Correct the Seasoning

Drain vegetables and chicken from the stock and place in serving bowl.

Add 3 Tbs.   BUTTER and permit to melt over them.

Use the stock for cooking rice, *Ugali*, or yams.

Kenya

KU KU PAKA | Coconut Chicken of Africa

It is customary to add 1 or 2 hot red peppers to this dish in Africa, but because of the delicacy of the coconut and the chicken, we suggest that *Pilli-pilli* be served with the dish separately. The recipe for *Pilli-pilli* is on page 128.

Yield: 8 portions

In a 6-quart Dutch oven or electric skillet:

Sauté	3 medium	ONIONS cut in ½-inch slices
	3	PEPPERS cut in ½-inch rings
	½ tsp.	GROUND GINGER
	1 tsp.	CURRY POWDER
	1 tsp.	SALT
	1 tsp.	SUGAR
	1 tsp.	GARLIC POWDER (or 3 cloves crushed)
	4 whole	CLOVES in

	2 oz.	OIL or MARGARINE until vegetables are soft.
Add	4 medium	TOMATOES cut in ½-inch slices and
	2 Tbs.	GRATED LEMON PEEL and cook for 2 minutes.
Add	2 3-lb.	FRYER CHICKENS cut into 8 pieces each.
Sauté	mixture about 5 minutes.	
Add	2 cups	COCONUT MILK (see page 226) and
	4 medium	POTATOES cut in 1- to 2-inch chunks.
Simmer	gently covered for 30 minutes until potatoes and chicken are done.	
Remove	the chicken pieces.	
Stir	the stew thoroughly but carefully so as not to break up vegetables.	
Ladle	the stew onto a serving platter and arrange the chicken on top. Sauce should be quite thick.	

Kenya

KARIOKOR NYAMA YA KUCHOMA | Barbecued Meat, Nairobi Market Style

Prepare the following combination and keep in a jar for barbecues:

½ cup	COARSE SALT (kosher type)
2 Tbs.	COARSE BLACK PEPPER
1 Tbs.	COARSE RED PEPPER
2 Tbs.	SUGAR
½ tsp.	GROUND GINGER.

This mixture is rubbed into the *fatty* parts of ribs, pork, or the skins of chicken with the fingers, and the meat is barbecued. Meats are never basted with sauces or oil, and yet they never seem to be dry. You might

Add 1 tsp.   GARLIC POWDER
       1 tsp.   ONION SALT.

However, if the meats you are using appear to be dry, keep a light salad oil on tap to brush on during the cooking if necessary.

Kenya

SAFARI STEAK FOR THE HUNTER

This is a recipe used by hunters on safari in preparing zebra, eland, antelope, or other game. The technique is good and gives us a new way to prepare our favorite food—beef steak.

Yield: 8 ½-lb. steaks

Buy	4 lbs.	STEAK (fillet, rump, or sirloin) cut into ½-lb. steaks each ½ inch thick and dry each steak completely with paper towels.

In an electric skillet or 10- to 12-inch skillet:

Heat	2 Tbs.	OIL and
	2 oz.	BUTTER, to the smoking point.

Fry steaks in pan a few at a time according to size of skillet for about 3 minutes on each side, adding fat as required.

Season each steak with salt and coarse-ground pepper and set aside in a warmer.

Lower heat and Add	1 cup	DRY RED WINE
	1 cup	SWEET (dessert) WINE.

Stir with the meat residues in the pan.

Add	2 cloves	GARLIC, finely minced.

Cook for 2 minutes.

Add	4 Tbs.	TOMATO PASTE thinned with
	4 Tbs.	WATER.

Cook until sauce is quite thick.

In a 2-quart saucepan:

Combine	3 cups	MASHED POTATOES and
	2 cups	MASHED YAMS or SWEET POTATOES and beat thoroughly.

Correct the Seasoning

Spread a bed of potatoes on a large platter.

Arrange the steaks on the potatoes.

Pour the sauce over the steaks.

Sprinkle with CHOPPED PARSLEY.

Tanzania

NYAMA YA FIGO | Beefsteak and Kidneys

In Dar Es Salaam, we had the good fortune to meet Jones Mayagola from Irinja, who is an excellent cook. He informed us that kidneys are considered a great delicacy in his part of the country and are always prepared with beef as in the recipe below.

Yield: 8 portions

Simmer	1	WHOLE BEEF KIDNEY in salted water to cover for about 30 minutes. Discard water. Cover again with water and simmer for about thirty minutes longer or until tender.
Sauté	1½ lbs. 2 oz.	ROUND STEAK cut into 1-inch pieces in BUTTER, lightly so as not to brown.
Add		BEEF KIDNEY, diced and sautéed for 1 to 2 minutes.
Add	1 tsp.	CURRY POWDER. Continue sautéeing.
Add	½ cup 2 1 pint 1 tsp. ½ tsp.	ONIONS, sliced TOMATOES, sliced WATER SALT CAYENNE PEPPER and cook for 15 to 20 minutes.
Serve with		UGALI and/or RICE and PILLI-PILLI (see page 128)

Nigeria

O JO JO MEAT BALLS

Yield: 24—48 balls

In a 2-quart bowl:

Combine	2 lbs. 2 1 medium 1 Tbs.	CHOPPED BEEF with GREEN BELL PEPPERS, chopped fine ONIONS, chopped fine SALT

½ lb.	WHITE POTATOES raw, peeled and grated
½ lb.	SWEET POTATOES raw, peeled and grated
3	EGGS.

Correct the Seasoning

Chill   thoroughly to set (at least 1 hour).

Form   into 2- or 3-inch balls.

Fry in   OIL until brown on all sides.

Serve   with desired vegetables at the side and PILLI-PILLI or a vegetable relish.

VEGETABLE MEAT BALLS

The secret here is grating RAW vegetables into chopped meat. This gives a light fluffy meat ball and is our favorite of all meat-ball recipes.

Yield: 8 portions

Combine	2 lbs.	CHUCK, freshly ground
	2 medium	POTATOES, peeled and grated raw
	2 medium	CARROTS, peeled and grated raw
	2 small	ONIONS, peeled and grated raw

Correct the Seasoning   with SALT and PEPPER.

Form   into balls, handling lightly, 1 to 2 inches in diameter and place on tray.

Chill   for 30 minutes.

Sauté   in margarine covering bottom of pan until lightly browned.

Cover with   TOMATO SAUCE or BROWN GRAVY.

Simmer   tightly covered for about 20 minutes until balls are thoroughly cooked.

BREADED MEAT BALLS

Imagine breading meat balls! But it is done in Nigeria and they are quite delicious. Chopped beef is blended with spices and eggs, formed into balls, dipped in bread crumbs, then in eggs thinned with water, and then in crumbs again. They are fried in oil on all sides.

Cameroon

CURRY OF BEEF CAMEROON | Beef with Pineapple and Coconut

Yield: 8 portions

In a 1-gallon Dutch oven or covered kettle:

Sauté	1 cup	YELLOW ONIONS, coarsely chopped with
	2 Tbs.	CURRY POWDER (use a good quality)
	2 Tbs.	SALT
	1 tsp.	BLACK PEPPER in
	½ cup	VEGETABLE OIL until onions are soft.
Add	4 lbs.	BONELESS CHUCK cut in 2-inch squares.

Cover pan immediately. Do not allow meat to brown.

Simmer for one hour slowly.

Add	½	FRESH PINEAPPLE trimmed and cut in 2-inch chunks
	½ cup	RAISINS.
Pierce	1	FRESH COCONUT and drain the water from it.

Add water to coconut water to make two cups and add to stew.

Simmer until meat is completely tender. About 1 hour.

Add	1	MANGO peeled and cut in long strips.

Add half the coconut cut into 1-inch squares or dominoes.

Cook for ten more minutes.

Correct the Seasoning If desired sprinkle with additional curry powder.

Cook	2 cups	RICE in
	5 cups	BOILING SALTED WATER.

Serve the curry over the rice with the following accompaniments in small bowls.
CHOPPED PEANUTS
CHOPPED HARD-BOILED EGGS
CHOPPED CUCUMBER
SHREDDED COCONUT
PINEAPPLE CHUTNEY (see page 192)
PILLI-PILLI SAUCE (see page 128).

Senegal

THIOU A LA VIANDE | Senegalese Beef Stew

The biggest bargain in Dakar was this stew everyone called "Chew." We found it in a tiny restaurant off on a side street seating just ten or twelve people, and the price was just 35 cents. Served in a huge enamel bowl, there was enough stew for three. It was delicious.

In a 4-quart Dutch oven:

Sauté	1 cup	CHOPPED ONIONS
	1 Tbs.	SALT
	½ tsp.	PEPPER, coarse-ground black
	¼ tsp.	THYME, whole
	¼ tsp.	CORIANDER in
	¼ cup	OIL, until onions are soft but not brown
Add	2 lbs.	STEW BEEF in ½-inch cubes.
Sauté	for 5 minutes on all sides.	
Combine	1 cup	TOMATO PASTE.
	3 cups	WATER
	½ cup	VINEGAR (white).
Simmer	with cover on until beef begins to become tender (about 1 hour).	
Add	½ lb.	WHITE POTATOES, cut in 2-inch cubes
	½ lb.	WHITE TURNIPS, cut in 2-inch cubes
	½ lb.	SWEET POTATOES, cut in 2-inch cubes
	8	CABBAGE WEDGES, 1 inch wide at bottom of wedge (about 1 lb.).
Sprinkle	lightly with SALT and PEPPER.	
Cover	and simmer slowly for 20 minutes.	
Arrange	1 lb.	COOKED RICE on large oval platter.
Place	meat and vegetables over the rice.	

South Africa

BOBOTIE | Chopped Beef in the Boer Manner

In South Africa, the *Bobotie* dish is decorated with lemon or bay leaves. Lemon slices or wedges may also be used.

Yield: 8 portions

	In a 4-quart saucepan:	
Sauté	1 cup	ONIONS, finely sliced with
	1	SOUR APPLE, peeled or diced in
	2 oz.	BUTTER, until onions are brown.
Blend in	2 lbs.	CHOPPED BEEF (or minced cooked beef)
	2	BREAD SLICES, soaked in
	½ cup	MILK and squeezed out
	2 Tbs.	CURRY POWDER
	½ cup	RAISINS (black)
	2 Tbs.	SLIVERED ALMONDS
	2 Tbs.	LEMON JUICE
	1	EGG
	½ tsp.	TURMERIC (optional).
Place	in a greased 12 x 7 x 2-inch baking dish.	
Insert	6	BAY LEAVES in an upright position with tips up, uniformly throughout the BOBOTIE.
Bake	for 40 minutes at 325° and remove from oven.	
Beat	1	EGG with
	½ cup	MILK and pour it over the BOBOTIE.
Bake	for 15 minutes longer.	
Remove	bay leaves before serving.	
Serve	with rice and chutney.	

Senegal

MAFFE AUX LÉGUMES ARACHID

Maffe is a beef or lamb stew made with *arachid* (peanut butter). It is one of the most popular entrées in Senegal.

Yield: 8 portions

		In a 1-gallon Dutch oven or heavy kettle:
Sauté	½ lb.	CHOPPED ONIONS in
	½ cup	OIL until onions are soft but not brown.
Add	2 lbs.	STEW BEEF or LAMB cut in 1-inch cubes.
Sauté		lightly until meat turns color but does not brown.
Add	1 6-oz. can	TOMATO PASTE, thinned with
	3 6-oz. cans	WATER or BEEF BROTH
	½ tsp.	CRUSHED RED PEPPER
	1 Tbs.	COARSE BLACK PEPPER
	1 Tbs.	SALT
	½ tsp.	THYME.
Cover		tightly and simmer over low heat for 1 hour or until meat is nearly done.
Add	8	CABBAGE WEDGES, 2 inches wide
	2 large	POTATOES, cut in quarters
	8 tiny	WHITE TURNIPS (whole)
	8 large	SWEET POTATOES, cut in halves.
Cover		and simmer for 30 minutes until vegetables are tender.
Place	1 cup	PEANUT BUTTER in a small bowl.
Pour		some of the pan gravy into the peanut butter to make a smooth cream.
Pour		peanut-butter mixture over the meat and vegetables.
Cook		for 5 minutes longer.
Cook	2 cups	RICE as package directs.
Place	½ cup	COOKED RICE in a large soup bowl.

Arrange	one of each vegetable around edge of bowl.
Stir up	mixture and place a ladleful of stew in center of plate.

Mauritania

PEPPER STEAK WITH COCONUT

Yield: 8 portions

Cut	3 lbs.	TENDERLOIN STEAK into ½-inch thick strips.
Crack	1	COCONUT, reserving the water. Remove dark skin with vegetable parer and cut coconut in strips same size as steak strips.
Slice	4	GREEN PEPPERS in strips same size as steak strips.
		In a 10-inch skillet:
Combine	½ cup	PEANUT or VEGETABLE OIL with
	1 Tbs.	SALT
	1 tsp.	BLACK PEPPER
	3 cloves	GARLIC, mashed (or 1 tsp. garlic powder)
	a few drops	TABASCO.
Sauté		the green peppers in the seasoned oil for 2 minutes.
Add		strips of steak and sauté for 2 minutes.
Add		strips of coconut and sauté for 2 minutes blending mixture together.
Add		water to the coconut water to make up 2 cups. Bring to a boil.
Add	2 Tbs.	SOY SAUCE
	2	BEEF BOUILLON CUBES.
Dissolve	4 Tbs.	CORNSTARCH in
	¼ cup	DRY VERMOUTH and add to the sauce.
Stir		over low heat until smooth and thickened to sauce consistency.
Pour		over the PEPPER STEAK.
Serve		with RICE BUJAMBURA (page 133).

Liberia

PALAVER SAUCE | Beef and Spinach

Palaver Sauce is actually not a sauce at all but a stew. In Ghana it is made with a combination of meats, fish, and greens with tomato paste and is called Palaver Sauce or Kontonmire Stew. The name itself has interesting origins; "Palaver" (or Palava in Ghana) means a long-winded debate or quarrel. It seems that the first Palava Sauces were made with greens which had long ropey stems. As a large group of people stood around the stew, the first to ladle out his portion would invariably slap his neighbor with one of the long stems, provoking a quarrel, and much talk and discussion would follow. The greens are now finely cut, but the name remains.

Yield: 8 portions

		In a 1-gallon pot:
Simmer	2 lbs.	STEW BEEF cut in ½-inch cubes (or use half beef and half chicken) in
	2 quarts	WATER and
	1 Tbs.	SALT until meat is half cooked.
Add	4 cups	COLLARD GREENS, chopped finely
	2 cups	SPINACH, chopped finely.
Simmer		gently until meat and greens are cooked (about 15 minutes).
Add	1 lb.	BONED SMOKED FISH.
Cook		for five minutes. All water should be absorbed.
Add	1 cup	ONIONS, chopped finely and sautéed lightly in
	½ cup	VEGETABLE or PEANUT OIL with
	1 or 2	small HOT PEPPERS (or 1 tsp. crushed red pepper).
Correct the Seasonings		
Simmer		five minutes longer.
Serve		with white rice.

Kenya

KIMA | Chopped Beef—Chili Fry

Chopped beef stew is very popular in East Africa—sautéed with lots of spices it is most tasty. Made with chili powder as the major ingredient, *Kima* is called "Chili Fry" (or Chilli-Fry). When it is made with curry it is called "Ground Meat Curry." In Africa very often meat or vegetable extract is added to improve the beef flavor and can be included here if desired.

Yield: 8 portions

In a 4-quart saucepan:

Sauté	1 cup	ONIONS, finely chopped
	1 tsp.	GARLIC POWDER ⎫ You may wish to decrease these
	1 tsp.	CURRY POWDER ⎬ amounts according to the hotness de-
	½ tsp.	CHILI POWDER ⎭ sired.
	1 tsp.	SALAD HERBS
	½ tsp.	BLACK PEPPER and
	1 cup	SHREDDED COCONUT in
	4 oz.	OIL or butter until onions are soft.
Add	2 lbs.	CHOPPED BEEF.
Sauté	until the meat turns brown.	
Add	½ cup	EVAPORATED MILK
	2 cups	WATER
	½ cup	TOMATO JUICE and
	¼ cup	LEMON JUICE.
Simmer	gently for 20 minutes.	
Correct the Seasonings		
Serve	in a large platter surrounded by RICE.	

Rhodesia

PINEAPPLE HAM WITH AVOCADO

Yield: 8 portions

In a 1-quart bowl:

Combine
- 2 cups — CRUSHED PINEAPPLE, canned
- ½ cup — BROWN SUGAR
- 2 Tbs. — PREPARED MUSTARD
- 1 tsp. — GROUND CLOVES.

Lay out on a baking sheet 8 ½-lb. HAM STEAKS, cut ½ inch thick, side by side.

Spread pineapple mixture uniformly over the ham steaks.

Bake at 350° for 20 minutes or until the pineapple has glazed the ham. (If mixture has not glazed enough, sprinkle with brown sugar and return to heat for 5 more minutes.)

Peel and Stone 2 ripe AVOCADOS.

Cut in uniform ½-inch slices.

Lift each ham steak onto dinner plates with a spatula.

Arrange 4 or 5 slices of avocado on each ham steak.

Serve with BAKED SWEET POTATOES in their jackets.

Uganda

CURRY OF VEAL WITH BANANAS

Cooked bananas give an interesting taste to any meat stew and are particularly good with the delicate flavor of veal. Treat them like a vegetable. Make certain that they are on the green side or they will fall apart in the cooking.

Yield: 8 portions

In a 4-quart saucepan:

Sauté 1 cup ONIONS, finely chopped

	1 Tbs.	CURRY POWDER
	1 tsp.	SALT
	¼ tsp.	PEPPER
	¼ tsp.	GINGER in
	2 oz.	MARGARINE or BUTTER until light brown.
Add	2 lbs.	VEAL (from shoulder) cut in 1-inch cubes.
Sauté		for 10 minutes.
Add	1 lb.	TOMATOES, cut in 1-inch wedges
	1 cup	WATER.
Simmer		for 30 minutes.
Add	4	BANANAS, peeled and cut in 2-inch lengths.
Simmer		for 15 minutes longer or until meat is done.

Correct the Seasoning

Pour into a 2-quart bowl.

Serve with a bowl of cooked WHITE RICE and a bowl of BRAISED CABBAGE (see page 63).

South Africa

GREEN BEAN BREDIE | Lamb Stew, South African Style

Bredie, or stew, is a typical meat dish which is always served in South Africa with rice. It can be made with any combination of vegetables but always includes mutton, preferably fat ribs. Since mutton is not generally available here, we have substituted lamb.

Yield: 8 portions

In a 4-quart heavy saucepan or Dutch oven:

Sauté 1 cup ONIONS, thinly sliced in

2 oz. MARGARINE until lightly brown.

Add	2 lbs.	LAMB (stewing) cut in 1-inch cubes.
Stir	over heat until lamb is browned on all sides.	
Add	2 cups	WATER
	2 tsp.	SALT
	¼ tsp.	PEPPER
	1	CHILI PEPPER cut in tiny pieces
	2 Tbs.	SUGAR.
Simmer	for 30 minutes covered.	
Spread	2 packages	REGULAR-CUT FROZEN STRING BEANS (thawed) over the meat and
	1 lb.	POTATOES, peeled and cut in ½-inch slices over beans.
Sprinkle with		SALT, PEPPER, and PAPRIKA.
Cover	tightly and simmer until vegetables are done.	
Serve	in a large bowl as a stew, with or without rice.	

Upper Volta

SPICED LAMB BALLS

West Africans are fond of meats, beans, and vegetables rolled into balls. Besides these Lamb Balls there are meat and bean balls, bean balls, *Akara* page 188, and meat balls page 173. The addition of spicy condiments makes them unusual and different from our own meat balls.

Yield: 32 balls

In a large skillet:

Sauté	1 cup	YELLOW ONIONS, chopped coarsely with
	½ tsp.	CINNAMON
	1 tsp.	POWDERED GINGER
	1 tsp.	GARLIC POWDER
	1 tsp.	CRUSHED RED PEPPERS
	1 tsp.	CORIANDER (powdered)
	1 tsp.	SALT in

	4 Tbs.	PEANUT OIL until onions are soft but not brown.
Cut	2 lbs.	COOKED LAMB (leftovers are fine) in 1-inch pieces and mix with the onion mixture.
Put		through the meat grinder once using a coarse blade.
Blend	3 large	EGGS beaten lightly and
	¼ cup	CRACKER or BREAD CRUMBS into mixture.
Form		into small 1-inch balls and dip in bread or cracker crumbs.
Chill		for 1 hour.
Deep-Fat Fry		at 375° until brown, about 4 minutes.
Spear		balls with toothpicks and place in a chafing dish.
Serve		with *Pilli-pilli* sauce.

FRITTERS

Fritters are very popular all over Africa and are used as a side dish as well as a dessert. These are side dishes.

Use a pancake mix or, if you prefer, use the following batter.

Sift	2 cups	ALL-PURPOSE FLOUR with
	2 tsp.	BAKING POWDER and
	1 tsp.	SALT.
Combine	2 large	EGGS beaten lightly with
	1½ cups	MILK and
	2 Tbs.	VEGETABLE OIL. Stir into the dry ingredients.

SWEET CORN FRITTERS

Add	2 cups	KERNEL CORN (drained) to above batter mixture.
Drop		by spoonfuls in deep fat at 375° until golden brown.

BANANA AND PEANUT FRITTERS

Add   3   BANANAS, cut in slices
          ½ cup   PEANUTS.

Drop   by spoonfuls in deep fat, fry at 375°, and cook until golden brown.

FRESH PINEAPPLE FRITTERS

Pare   1   PINEAPPLE, core and cut into ¾-inch slices, then in quarters.

Dip   in above batter and proceed as Banana Fritters.

To save time use a good pancake mix. Adjust the quantity of liquid as necessary .

OKRA FRITTERS

Add   2 cups   COOKED OKRA cut in 1-inch pieces (drained).

Proceed   as Sweet Corn Fritters.

Tanzania

YELLOW COCONUT RICE

This is rich but really delicious! You may, if you like, add ½ cup grated coconut to give it a stronger coconut flavor.

Yield: 8 portions

In a 2-quart saucepan:

Prepare   2 cups   COCONUT MILK (see page 226).

Add   3 cups   MILK and bring to boiling point.

Add   2 cups   RICE
          1 tsp.   SALT

½ tsp.	GROUND TURMERIC
¼ tsp.	GROUND CINNAMON
¼ tsp.	GROUND CLOVES
¼ tsp.	GROUND CARDAMOM (optional).

Cover   and cook until rice is absorbed, about 20 minutes.

Add   2 Tbs.   BUTTER.

Serve   as vegetable with fish or chicken.

West Africa

CORN AND BEANS | African Succotash

Corn, known to the Africans as Maize or Mealies, is used in countless ways: pounded into corn flour, cornstarch, and cornmeal or cooked whole and cut from the cob.

The Africans combine corn with other starchy products such as rice, beans, and mashed potatoes as in *Irio,* the national dish of Kenya (see page 52), and as in this African succotash.

A few corn ideas from Africa:

Corn and Plantain Stew: Equal parts kernel corn and plantains. Cook together until tender.

Corn and Fish Chowder: Add green peppers and tomatoes for color and flavor to any fish or seafood chowder.

Maize Stew: Add chopped shrimp and hard-boiled eggs to corn and bean dish above.

Yield: 8 portions

In a 4-quart saucepan:

Sauté

½ cup	ONIONS, chopped finely
½ cup	GREEN or RED BELL PEPPERS, chopped finely
1 tsp.	SALT
½ tsp.	COARSE RED PEPPER
¼ tsp.	PEPPER
½ tsp.	CURRY POWDER (optional) in
¼ cup	OIL until light brown.

Add	1 cup	DRIED WHITE BEANS or PEAS and
	1 quart	BOILING WATER.
Simmer		for 1 to 1½ hours until beans are cooked.
Add	2 cups	KERNEL CORN (CANNED).
Correct the seasoning		
Cook		for 10 minutes longer.
Drain		excess liquid if any.
Add	1 oz.	BUTTER
Serve		as a vegetable accompaniment for meat, fish, or poultry.

Nigeria

AKARA | Bean Balls

Pulses (dried peas, beans and lentils) are the most important part of the diet of the West African and *Akara* is, perhaps, the most popular dish. *Akara* is also served as a snack or as a dessert with fried bananas or plantains.

Yield: about 20 balls

In a 1-quart bowl:

Soak	1 lb.	DRIED WHITE BEANS or BLACK-EYED PEAS in water overnight.
Drain		and remove any loose skins and put through a meat grinder.
Add	½ tsp.	CAYENNE PEPPER
	1 tsp.	SALT
	½	ONION finely chopped.
Beat		in enough warm water to give beans consistency so that mixture drops easily from spoon.

In a 9-inch skillet:

Drop	by teaspoons in hot fat and fry until golden brown on both sides.
Serve	as a side vegetable.

There are many variations for making AKARA. Following the same method as above you can:

Add ½ cup cooked AKARA to 1 cup cooked okra or
Add grated cheese to the AKARA mixture.

East Africa

NDIZI | Steamed Bananas (or Plantains)

Steamed unsweetened bananas are served as a starchy vegetable in many countries of Africa. You may want to sprinkle on some brown sugar but don't make it too sweet if it is to accompany a meat dish.

Banana leaves may be purchased in specialty fruit shops or Puerto Rican or Mexican markets which often carry them. If banana leaves are not available you may cook the bananas in aluminum foil, folded over the bananas as described below. If you are using foil, they may be baked in the oven at 375° for 45 minutes.

Yield: 8 portions

Line a 4-quart pan (with heavy cover) with

	4 to 6	BANANA LEAVES so they overlap the pan and cover bottom completely.
Place	8	BANANAS, rather green (or plantains), peeled but left whole, side by side in the pan.
Sprinkle with	1 tsp.	SALT and
	½ cup	BROWN SUGAR (optional).
Lap		the banana leaves over the bananas to obtain a tight seal.
Pour	1 cup	WATER at side of pan as it goes *under* the leaves.
Cover		tightly and simmer slowly for 1 hour.
Remove		leaves.
Arrange		bananas on a 10-inch serving platter.
Dribble with	2 oz.	MELTED BUTTER.
Serve		as a vegetable.

Tanzania

BAKED BANANAS

When bananas are served as an accompaniment in Tanzania, they are rarely sweetened. We might find the bananas to be quite tasteless without the addition of a little sugar. Try them both ways—and you will find they are a most adaptable food.

Yield: 8 portions

On a cookie sheet or shallow baking pan:

Place	4 large	BANANAS, unpeeled with ends cut off.
Bake		at 425° for 15 minutes or until skin bursts and turns black.
Turn		bananas over and bake on the other side for 5 minutes.
Peel		the skins and cut the bananas in two.
Pour	1 tsp.	MELTED BUTTER over each banana.
Sprinkle with	1 tsp. 1 tsp.	BROWN SUGAR and LEMON JUICE.
Arrange		carefully on a small platter.

BATTER-FRIED BANANAS

Yield: 8 portions

In a 1-quart bowl:

Prepare	1 cup	PANCAKE MIX following package directions using enough liquid to form a thin consistency.
Cut	4 large	PEELED BANANAS once lengthwise and once crosswise.
Dip		the bananas in the batter.

In a medium skillet:

Sauté	each in enough hot oil to cover bottom of pan until bananas are golden brown on both sides.
Arrange	on a small platter attractively.

West Africa

DUNDU ONIYERI | Fried Yams

Yams are almost as important in the African diet as rice—especially on the West Coast. This delicious root vegetable is prepared in so many ways, one could do a whole book on it alone. The most common types are the orange-yellow yam which we have here, and the white yam from which *Foo-foo* is made. Yams are boiled, mashed, pounded into flour, made into balls, fritters, soups, and sauces. Yams are often a part of stews—the most popular is called Palm Oil Chop.

Yam Potato Chips are a popular dessert.

Yam Chips: Slice yams thin as potato chips—deep fry at 375° quickly.

Yam Soup: Follow recipe for any chicken soup. Add enough yams to give it body (1 lb. per 2 quarts of stock). Purée the soup for a new flavor sensation.

Yield: 8 servings

In a 2-quart saucepan:

Cover 2 lbs. YAMS (or sweets) peeled and cut in uniform ½-inch slices with
1 quart WATER and
1 tsp. SALT.

Cook until tender and drain. Shake over heat to dry out.

For seasoned flour:

Combine 1 cup FLOUR
1 tsp. SALT
½ tsp. BLACK PEPPER
½ tsp. CINNAMON
½ tsp. PAPRIKA.

Dip yams in seasoned flour, then in following egg mixture:

Beat 2 EGGS lightly with
2 Tbs. WATER.

Dip in the flour again.

Deep-Fat Fry at 360° or sauté in oil until golden brown and serve very hot as a vegetable or side dish.

East Africa

HORSERADISH RELISH SAUCE

This relish is very popular in Tanzania and generally in East Africa. It can be used as a sauce over boiled beef or as a relish with any bland meat.

Yield: 1 pint

In a 1-quart saucepan:

Sauté	¼ cup	ONIONS, very thinly sliced, and
	1	TOMATO, cut in half and thinly sliced, in
	2 oz.	BUTTER until soft but not brown.
Add	1 cup	GRATED WHITE HORSERADISH (bottled)
	1 cup	COCONUT MILK (see page 225)
	½ tsp.	TURMERIC.
Cook	for 10 minutes.	
Add	2 Tbs.	CORNSTARCH dissolved in
	2 Tbs.	WATER.
Cook	until slightly thickened.	
Serve	1 to 2 Tbs. hot or cold as a sauce over meats or poultry.	

Zambia

PINEAPPLE CHUTNEY

Use this chutney with any of the meat dishes as well as with curries.

Yield: 2 quarts

In a 1-gallon saucepan:

Combine	1 cup	GREEN PEPPER, in ¾-inch cubes
	½ cup	ONIONS, chopped in ½-inch pieces
	1 lb.	FRESH TOMATOES, in ¾-inch cubes
	1	WHOLE LEMON, cut in ½-inch cubes with skin left on
	1	WHOLE ORANGE, cut in ½-inch cubes with skin left on
	½ cup	BLACK SEEDED RAISINS

1 cup	FRESH PINEAPPLE, in ½-inch dice (or use canned tidbits)
1 cup	WHITE VINEGAR
½ cup	WHITE SUGAR
½ cup	DARK BROWN SUGAR
4 Tbs.	PRESERVED CANDIED GINGER, cut in thin strips
1 Tbs.	SALT.

Simmer gently for 30 minutes. If mixture appears thick, add 1 cup pineapple juice. One teaspoon powdered ginger may be used in place of the preserved ginger.

Pack in hot sterile jars.

Niger

MANGO SALAD

Any yellow melon such as canteloupe or Spanish melon may be used if mangos are not available.

Yield: 8 servings

In a 2-quart bowl:

Cut	2	MANGOS in ½-inch cubes in a 2-quart bowl.
Add	½	FRESH PINEAPPLE cut in ½-inch cubes.
Blend	½ cup	LEMON JUICE with
	1 cup	APRICOT NECTAR or ORANGE JUICE.

Pour juices over fruit.

Serve on LETTUCE CUPS individually or in a bowl.

Garnish with 2 or 3 FRESH STRAWBERRIES per salad.

For a variation on this salad, peel 4 avocados, cut them in half, and remove the stones. Fill with the above mango mixture and serve on a lettuce bed. Or you may alternate long slices of mango (or melon) with watermelon and grapefruit sections and serve with Jungle Salad Dressing (page 134).

East Africa

M'CHICHA | Spinach

The addition of chopped peanuts to the spinach gives it a delightful crunchiness, the grated coconut an unexpected flavor.

SPINACH AND GROUNDNUTS

Yield: 8 portions

In a 2-quart saucepan:

Melt 2 oz.   BUTTER

Add   2 12-oz.
packages   THAWED FROZEN CHOPPED SPINACH
½ cup   GRATED COCONUT and
½ cup   PEANUTS chopped finely.

Toss lightly until ingredients are combined, heated through, and all liquid is absorbed.

Correct the Seasoning with SALT and PEPPER.

Serve as a vegetable with any meat, poultry, or fish entrée.

SPINACH SAUTÉ AND GROUNDNUTS

In a 2-quart saucepan:

Sauté ½ cup   ONIONS chopped finely in
2 oz.   BUTTER or MARGARINE until lightly brown.

Add 1 cup   PEANUTS very finely chopped, or ground.

Sauté until peanuts and onions are quite brown.

Add 2 packages   THAWED FROZEN CHOPPED SPINACH

Sauté all together lightly until liquid is absorbed.

**Correct the
Seasoning** with SALT and a few drops of TABASCO.

Serve with poached or scrambled eggs.

Zanzibar

BAMIA LADYFINGER RELISH

"Ladyfingers" is the African name for okra and a fitting one for a delicate vegetable that we do not use nearly enough. Of course, the relish is best if made with fresh okra. The canned okra is a compromise but it does make a new and different relish to add to your menu.

Yield: 1 quart

In an electric skillet or large frying pan:

Sauté	½ cup	ONION, thinly sliced, in
	2 Tbs.	OIL until slightly brown.
Chop	½ cup	ONIONS
	2 cloves	GARLIC
	1	CHILI PEPPER (or use 1 tsp. crushed red pepper)
	1 inch	FRESH GINGER (or use 1 tsp. ground ginger).

Add to oil and sauté for 1 minute.

Add 2 lbs. FRESH OKRA, trimmed at ends and cut in 1-inch slices (or drain two 16-oz. cans of okra).

Sauté for several minutes.

Add 1 FRESH TOMATO cut in thin strips.

Sauté for 5 minutes.

Pack into hot sterile jar.

Serve hot or cold with meats and fish as a side relish.

Spanish Morocco

LIMONES Y ACEITUNAS EN ESCABECHE | Pickled Lemons and Olives Tetuan

Pickled lemons and pickled olives are served in separate dishes but always together. What a nice change from the usual plain black olives to pickled black olives. And just think of pickled lemons! We are grateful to Spanish Morocco for these contributions to African fare.

In a 1-quart jar:

Place	8	LEMONS, each washed and cut in 8 wedges
	3 Tbs.	SALT
	½ cup	VINEGAR
	½ cup	SALAD OIL and
		WATER to fill jar.

In a second 1-quart jar:

Place	3 cups	BLACK OLIVES, canned
	3 Tbs.	SALT
	½ cup	VINEGAR
	½ cup	SALAD OIL and
		WATER to fill jar.

Cover jars.

Keep at room temperature for 1 week and then refrigerate until ready to use.

Serve with meat and fish or poultry as a relish.

Ivory Coast

CUCUMBER-ZUCCHINI SALAD

Yield: salad bowl for 8

In a 2-quart bowl:

Arrange in alternate layers	2 medium	CUCUMBERS, scored with a fork, not peeled but sliced very thinly
	2 medium	ZUCCHINI, raw, same size as cucumbers, prepared the same way.
Blend	½ cup	WHITE VINEGAR with
	4 Tbs.	SUGAR dissolved in
	1 cup	HOT WATER
	1 Tbs.	SALT
	1 tsp.	COARSE BLACK PEPPER (fresh ground if available)
	1 tsp.	CRUSHED RED PEPPER.

Drain any water formed from cucumbers before adding the dressing.

Allow vegetables to marinate in the dressing at least 1 hour before serving.

Serve with meat, fish, or poultry.

Note that no oil is used in the above dressing. The amount of sugar is not excessive for this kind of dressing. An artificial sweetener may be substituted for the sugar if desired.

In Africa many raw vegetables are used in salads. To tossed greens you can add raw cauliflower, young fresh broccoli, very fresh string beans, cut in small pieces, raw carrot rings, zucchini, or any fresh young squash. Or you may cut bits of yellow cheese and anchovies into your green salad as well as the raw vegetables. Always add thin slices of Bermuda onion.

West Africa

CABBAGE AND PINEAPPLE SALAD

Yield: 8 small salads or a 2-quart salad bowl

Shred in thin slivers	1 lb.	YOUNG CABBAGE (or Chinese cabbage).
Lift		a handful of cabbage at a time and from a 12-inch height allow the cabbage to drop lightly into a 2-quart bowl.
Add	1 cup	CELERY, cut diagonally (Chinese cut)
	½ cup	GREEN PEPPERS, in thin strips
	½ cup	TOMATOES, in tiny wedges
	1 cup	FRESH PINEAPPLE, in ½-inch dice
	1 tsp.	SALT
	1 grind of	FRESHLY GRATED PEPPER
	1 tsp.	SALAD HERBS.
Blend		in lightly the following dressing:
Combine	1 cup	YOGURT with
	2 Tbs.	SOUR CREAM
	2 to 3 Tbs.	MILK.
Beat		together until consistency of heavy cream.
Add		only enough dressing to hold the salad together.
Serve		in small wooden salad bowls or one large bowl for the table.
Garnish		with parsley or watercress.

West Africa

CUCUMBER BOAT STUFFED WITH FLAKED FISH SALAD

Yield: 8 salads

Peel	4 medium	CUCUMBERS in strips ½-inch apart.
Cut		each in half lengthwise to give eight halves (or one half per person).
Cut		out soft centers with a grapefruit knife. Chop and set aside.
Cut		a strip from bottom of cucumber half so that it will rest firmly on the plate.
		In a 2-quart bowl:
Combine	2 cups	COLD FLAKED FISH as halibut, bass, etc. (or use canned tuna or salmon)
	½ cup	CELERY in ½-inch pieces and
	all the	CHOPPED CUCUMBER scooped from "boats."
Blend	½ cup	SOUR CREAM with
	4 Tbs.	LEMON JUICE
	2 Tbs.	SUGAR
	½ tsp.	SALT.
Add		to fish mixture, blend well, and chill.
Shred	1 head	LETTUCE in long thin slivers to simulate "waves."
Arrange		on dinner or large salad plates.
Place		the cucumber boat on the lettuce.
Heap		the fish mixture to fill the cucumber shells.
Cut	1 slice	AMERICAN CHEESE in half diagonally to form a "sail." Place in the center of mixture, narrow edge upright.
Cut a tiny banner of	1	PIMIENTO piece ½ inch × 1½ inches and pin it to the center of narrow side of cheese with a piece of toothpick.
Garnish around edge with	2 or 3	TOMATO SLICES and PARSLEY SPRIGS.

South Africa

AVOCADO STUFFED WITH SEAFOOD

Yield: 8 portions

		In a 1-quart bowl:
Blend	¼ cup	LEMON JUICE
	¼ cup	DRY WHITE WINE
	1 tsp.	CURRY POWDER
	½ tsp.	MACE.
Add	1 pint	MAYONNAISE.
Mix	1 lb.	CRABMEAT or LOBSTER MEAT
	½ lb.	SHRIMP, cleaned and deveined.

Marinate the seafood slightly with a little of the dressing immediately before serving. Use only enough dressing to blend.

Arrange		LETTUCE leaves to form cups on plates.
Place		AVOCADO halves, peeled, in center of cup.
Fill	lightly with seafood blended with dressing.	
Arrange	4	GRAPEFRUIT SECTIONS at side of plate.
Place	1 strip of	PIMIENTO across grapefruit.
Place	2 sprigs	CHICORY, one at each end of grapefruit.
Top with	1	BLACK OLIVE.
Garnish with	½	HARD-BOILED EGG.
Top with	3 or 4	CAPERS
	2	CARROT CURLS, one at each side.

East Africa

TOMATO ROSE STUFFED WITH CHICKEN AND PINEAPPLE SALAD

Yield: 8 salads

In a 2-quart bowl:

Combine	2 cups	COOKED CHICKEN in ½-inch cubes
	1 cup	CANNED PINEAPPLE CHUNKS, drained.
Blend	½ cup	MAYONNAISE with
	½ tsp.	CURRY POWDER
	2 Tbs.	CRYSTALLIZED GINGER chopped finely.

Combine all but a few tablespoons of the ginger mayonnaise with chicken and pineapple.

Chill.

Cut 1 to 2 heads LETTUCE and shape into eight uniform cups on dinner plates.

Remove stems from

8   TOMATOES. Make six even cuts from the blossom end three-quarters of the way through each tomato. Do not cut through. Open out to form a rose.

Place tomato rose in center of each lettuce bed.

Fill tomatoes with mixture. (Use a scoop if available.)

Place 1 tsp.   GINGER MAYONNAISE on top of mixture.

Garnish with 1   BLACK OLIVE and

1 or 2

sprigs   WATERCRESS or PARSLEY.

Arrange 6 to 8   PLANTAIN CHIPS at side of plate.

Ivory Coast

SUMMER-DAY SALAD BOWL

Yield: 8 large salad bowls

In a 2-quart bowl:

Combine	3 cups	COOKED COLD RICE
	1 cup	COOKED HAM in ½-inch cubes
	1 cup	COOKED CHICKEN in ½-inch cubes
	½ cup	CELERY in ¼-inch pieces
	2	PIMIENTOS (canned) in ¼-inch pieces
	1 cup	PINEAPPLE or MELON or both
	2 Tbs.	SHREDDED COCONUT
	2 Tbs.	CHOPPED PEANUTS
	1 tsp.	SALT.
Blend	1 cup	MAYONNAISE with
	3 Tbs.	FROZEN ORANGE JUICE CONCENTRATE, undiluted.
Combine	¾ cup of orange mayonnaise with the mixture.	
Line	wooden salad bowls using	
	1 to 2	
	heads	LETTUCE.
Divide	mixture among the bowls.	
Garnish top of salad with	1 to 2 Tbs.	ORANGE MAYONNAISE.
Sprinkle	1 tsp.	CHOPPED PEANUTS on the mayonnaise.
Decorate with		WATERCRESS or PARSLEY SPRIGS.

AFRICAN FRUIT SALAD

This salad or comparable greens and fruit combinations are served in all parts of Africa. The salad is ideal for a group of women on any occasion and men also appreciate it on a hot day. It is especially appropriate for a weekend or outdoor luncheon.

Yield: 8 wooden salad bowls

In a 2-gallon bowl:

Stem, Wash, and Tear into medium-sized pieces	2 quarts	RAW SPINACH
	2 quarts	ROMAINE
	1 quart	CHICORY
	1 quart	LETTUCE

Fill the bowls with the mixture of greens.

Use any fresh fruits, coconut, and chopped peanuts in combinations like this:

1	FRESH PINEAPPLE cut in fingers, about 3 per bowl
1	FRESH MANGO in strips, about 2–3 per bowl
1	AVOCADO, dipped in lemon juice and cut in strips
1	FRESH COCONUT, cut in thin slices
4	ORANGES (California type), thinly sliced with skins left on
3	BANANAS, cut in chunks, thinly coated with MAYONNAISE and dipped in CHOPPED PEANUTS (or coconut)
1 pint-basket	STRAWBERRIES or any berries in season.

Arrange the fruits attractively in the individual salad bowls or in one large bowl.

Serve with LIME DRESSING:

Grate

4	LIMES, and add grated rinds with their juice to
1 quart	MAYONNAISE.

Fold in

1 cup	WHIPPED CREAM sweetened with
2 Tbs.	SUGAR
few drops	GREEN VEGETABLE COLORING.

Tanzania

MEAT SAMOSAS | The African Hamburger

Yield: 12 *Samosas*

	In a 1-quart bowl:
Combine	2 cups FLOUR, sifted, with water to make a stiff dough.
Knead	until smooth and divide in 4 parts.
Roll	each piece into a circle 4 inches in diameter on a board.
Brush	each with COOKING OIL
Sprinkle	evenly with flour.
Place	the circles on top of each other with floured sides facing.
Gently Roll	pile of circles into large circle 8 to 9 inches in diameter. (Note: at beginning pastry should be turned over while rolling to make all circles same size.)

On iron grill or flat Teflon pan:

Fry	pastry on both sides without browning it (about 2 minutes on each side). (Large and small bubbles will swell up pastry indicating when done.)
Cool	slightly.
Cut	pastry in three uniform strips and peel off pieces. There are now twelve strips.

In a 1-quart saucepan:

Combine	1 lb.	COOKED MEAT (beef or lamb), ground or finely minced
	1 clove	GARLIC, mashed
	1 tsp.	SALT
	1 tsp.	MINT LEAVES, dried
	½ cup	CHOPPED ONIONS
	¼ tsp.	CINNAMON
	¼ tsp.	GINGER
	¼ tsp.	CLOVES
	¼ tsp.	CHILI POWDER
	4 Tbs.	LEMON JUICE.

Cook	mixture for 10 minutes stirring constantly. Cool.
Make	a cone at one end of the pastry strip.

Hold	the cone in left hand and fill with mixture.
Turn	the flap over to form a three-cornered pastry.
Seal	the edge with a paste made with 1 Tbs. FLOUR and 1 Tbs. WATER.
Chill	for 1 hour.
Deep-Fat Fry	at 375° until golden brown.
Serve	with LEMON WEDGES while still hot.

As an adaptation, you can make *Samosas* with pie crust. Purchase the packaged mix and bake the *Samosas*. Or in making your own pie crust cut down on shortening by half for deep-fat frying.

Liberia

LIBERIAN RICE BREAD NO. 1

This rice bread is the typical recipe used by the Liberian housewife. It is not too sweet, can be used as a coffee cake or as a bread, and stays moist for a full week.

Yield: 8 × 12-inch bread

In a 4-quart bowl:

Combine	2 cups	CREAM OF RICE (cereal)
	3 cups	MASHED BANANAS
	½ cup	VEGETABLE OIL
	4 Tbs.	SUGAR
	½ tsp.	NUTMEG
	1 tsp.	SALT
	1 cup	WATER
	1 tsp.	BAKING SODA.
Stir	until thoroughly blended.	
Bake	in a well-greased 8 × 12-inch rectangular or 9-inch round cake pan at 400° for 30 minutes.	
Test	with a toothpick (when it comes out dry, bread is done).	

LIBERIAN RICE BREAD

This is a slightly richer bread and resembles our banana cake.

In a 4-quart bowl:

Combine
- 2 cups   CREAM OF RICE (cereal)
- 4 Tbs.   SUGAR
- 4 tsp.   BAKING POWDER
- 1 tsp.   SALT.

Stir in
- 2 cups   MASHED BANANAS
- 2   LARGE EGGS
- 1 cup   MILK
- ½ cup   VEGETABLE OIL.

Bake in a well-greased 8 × 12-inch rectangular or 9-inch round cake pan at 375° for 45 minutes.

Test with a toothpick as above.

Liberia

PINEAPPLE NUT BREAD

The women of Liberia are excellent bakers. Pineapple Nut Bread is a favorite. This bread cuts better on the second day, so plan to make it a day ahead. Slice it thinly and serve with cream cheese. It's a great change from our usual date-nut bread.

Yield: 10-inch loaf

In a 4-quart bowl:

Combine
- 2½ cups   ALL-PURPOSE FLOUR
- 1 cup   BRAN
- 1 Tbs.   BAKING POWDER
- 1 tsp.   BAKING SODA
- 1 tsp.   SALT
- ½ cup   CHOPPED ROASTED PEANUTS (or WALNUTS).

Beat 2   EGGS until light.

Add ¾ cup   CRUSHED PINEAPPLE, drained.

Add wet ingredients to dry and stir thoroughly.

Bake at 350° in greased loaf pan for 1 hour. Test with toothpick. (When toothpick is dry, bread is done.)

West Africa

GROUNDNUT BREAD

Yield: 12 1½- to 2-inch pieces

Prepare 1 package   ROLL MIX (follow package instructions)

Roll out on a floured board to ½-inch thickness.

Spread 1 cup   PEANUT BUTTER uniformly over the surface.

Roll up tightly.

Holding index finger at one end of roll, swing the roll around to form a round loaf.

Lift the round loaf onto a greased cookie sheet pan with a spatula.

Allow to rise as directed on the package.

Brush 2 Tbs.   MELTED BUTTER over loaf.

Sprinkle 4 Tbs.   CHOPPED PEANUTS over top, pressing them into loaf.

Score across the top of loaf with a knife, with lines 1 inch apart for criss-cross effect.

Bake as directed on package for a full loaf.

Break or cut into 1½- to 2-inch pieces when serving.

A quick way to prepare a bread popular with children resembling the Groundnut Bread is the following:

Cut a long French or Italian loaf in 2-inch slices without cutting through the bread. Spread the slices with peanut butter. Wrap the loaf tightly in aluminum foil and heat at 375° for 5 minutes. Remove the foil. Spread the loaf thinly with peanut butter (across top) and sprinkle with chopped peanuts.

Nigeria

PUFF-PUFF | Fried Bread

West Africans are fond of fried breads and cookies such as *Puff-puff* and *Chin-chin* (see page 135). *Puff-puff* is most often eaten as a plain bread but many variations are possible, especially when it is made for a dessert. You can experiment with various condiments, such as allspice, nutmeg, cinnamon, etc.

Yield: 3 dozen from a 13¾-oz. package

Follow directions for	1 package	ROLL MIX for making bread.
	Before adding liquid as directed on package,	
Add	1 tsp. 2 Tbs.	SALAD HERBS CHOPPED PARSLEY.
After	dough has risen as directed, form into 1-inch balls.	
Deep-fat fry	at 360° until golden brown and puffy.	

DOUGHNUTS, AFRICAN STYLE

Follow directions	1 package	ROLL MIX as above
	Before adding liquid as directed on package,	
Add	½ cup 1 Tbs. 4 Tbs.	SUGAR VANILLA SHREDDED COCONUT.
After	dough has risen as directed, form into 1-inch balls.	
Deep-Fat Fry	at 360° until golden brown and puffy.	
Sprinkle with		CONFECTIONERS' SUGAR.

Tanzania

CHAPATIS | Bread of East Africa

Chapatis should be light and flaky. Keep them lightly covered before serving. They may be quickly warmed in a hot oven before going on the table or served cold. They are a breakfast or afternoon tea accompaniment and excellent spread with butter or jelly.

Yield: 8 *Chapatis*

In a 3-quart bowl:

Sift	1 cup	ALL-PURPOSE FLOUR
	½ tsp.	SALT.
Blend in	1 cup	WATER to make a fairly stiff dough.
Knead	thoroughly with the fingertips.	
Roll	into a round circle on a floured board.	
Brush	the surface with oil.	
Cut	once from the center of the circle to the edge.	
Roll	the pastry into a cone.	
Press	both ends in and form into a ball again.	
Brush	with oil and repeat process twice more.	
Divide	the pastry into 1-oz. balls and roll each thinly into a 5- to 6-inch circle with a rolling pin.	
Heat	a small frying pan or skillet.	
Place	1 Tbs.	OIL in pan and fry each round of *Chapati* separately on both sides until golden brown, adding oil as required.
Serve	with entrées as a bread.	

Africa

COCONUT ICE CREAM BALL IN STRAWBERRY-PINEAPPLE SAUCE

Spoon out 8 3-inch
scoops VANILLA ICE CREAM, rounding them to make large balls.

Roll the balls quickly in SHREDDED COCONUT until completely coated.

Place on a small tray side by side and refreeze.

In a 1-quart bowl:

Combine 1 8-oz. jar STRAWBERRY JAM and
1 8-oz. jar PINEAPPLE JAM.

Thin to sauce consistency with
¼ to ½
cup ANY SWEET WINE or BRANDY.

Place 3 to 4 Tbs. sauce in bottom of compote dish.

"Sit" the coconut ball in the sauce.

FOOLS

The term "fool" (also the Egyptian word for lentils) comes from the English and means essentially a fruit purée folded into a soft custard or whipped cream. You may begin with any good custard recipe, vanilla pudding, or whipped cream. Use one part custard or cream to one part puréed, mashed, or cut fruit. Below are three Fools from Ghana, Liberia, and Nigeria.

Ghana

Strawberry Fool

Yield: 8 ½-cup servings

In a 1-quart bowl:

Sprinkle ¼ cup CONFECTIONERS' SUGAR over
1 cup STRAWBERRIES cut in quarters.

In a 1-quart bowl:

Beat   1 cup   HEAVY CREAM with
          3–4 Tbs.   PORT or MADEIRA WINE
          ¼ cup   CONFECTIONERS' SUGAR, until stiff.

Fold   whipped cream into strawberries.

Pile   high in footed sherbet glasses.

Garnish   each with one whole strawberry.

Liberia

Peach Fool

Yield: 8 ½-cup servings

In a 2-quart bowl:

Fold   2 cups   STEWED PEACHES (drained, puréed, and cooled) into
          2 cups   CUSTARD, boiled, or VANILLA PUDDING (from a mix) cooled
                     to room temperature.

Nigeria

Peanut Fool

Yield: 8 healthy servings

In a 2-quart double boiler:

Dissolve   1 cup   PEANUT BUTTER in
          3½ cups   MILK with
          ½ cup   SUGAR.

Stir   thoroughly and heat to scalding point.

Add to   5 large   EGGS beaten slightly.

Return   to double boiler and cook over hot water until mixture coats the spoon.

Place   2 Tbs.   CHOPPED PEANUTS in bottom of champagne glasses.

Pour   the custard over the peanuts and chill.

Top   with WHIPPED CREAM or MERINGUE sprinkled with chopped peanuts.

Africa

ORANGE-CHOCOLATE PARFAIT "L'AFRIQUE"

Yield: 1 serving

In a whiskey-sour glass:

Place	2 Tbs.	CHOCOLATE SAUCE
	1 scoop	CHOCOLATE ICE CREAM
	1 scoop	RASPBERRY SHERBET
	1 scoop	ORANGE SHERBET
Add	2 Tbs.	CHOCOLATE SAUCE.
Top with		WHIPPED CREAM and
	2	MANDARIN ORANGE SLICES as a garnish.

RAINBOW PARFAIT

It is my belief that parfaits are best made to order. If you must prepare ahead of time, freeze before adding the whipped cream.

Yield: 1 serving

In a tall cold parfait glass:

Place	2 Tbs.	STRAWBERRIES or RASPBERRIES fresh or frozen and thawed
	1 small scoop	RASPBERRY SHERBET
	1 small scoop	LIME SHERBET
	3 Tbs.	STRAWBERRIES or RASPBERRIES
	1 small scoop	VANILLA ICE CREAM to fill glass to the brim.
Swirl		WHIPPED CREAM on top. (If you're ambitious use a pastry bag to make a large star.)
Garnish whipped cream with		MULTICOLORED SPRINKLES or CHOCOLATE SPRINKLES (purchased at grocery store).
Serve	immediately.	

Africa

LEOPARD ICE CREAM

Experiment with combinations of ice creams to obtain interesting effects and use unusual stemmed glasses (such as bar glasses) for serving. Here are some ideas:

Soften	1 quart	FRENCH VANILLA ICE CREAM until it is in a workable but not melted state.
Fold in	1 cup	PEANUT BUTTER, blending in 1 tsp. at a time to give the effect of leopard spots.
Refreeze		

MANGO ICE CREAM

Soften	1 quart	FRENCH VANILLA ICE CREAM as above
Fold in	1 cup	MANGOS, cut in thin, 2-inch-long slices to give stripe effect.
Refreeze		

CINNAMON-COCONUT-SWIRL ICE CREAM

Soften	1 quart	FRENCH VANILLA ICE CREAM as above.
Fold in	2 Tbs. 1 cup	CINNAMON and SHREDDED COCONUT, streaking both through the ice cream.
Refreeze		

AVOCADO ICE CREAM

Soften	1 quart	PISTACHIO ICE CREAM as above.
Fold in	2 cups	AVOCADO cut in ½-inch cubes or slices. A striking contrast.
Refreeze		

Gabon

BAKED BANANAS GABON

Cut	8	BANANAS in three uniformly diagonal pieces.
Beat	1	EGG lightly with
	2 Tbs.	ORANGE JUICE.
Dip		bananas in egg mixture, then in
	½ cup	BREAD CRUMBS.
Heat	½ cup	VEGETABLE OIL in a sauté pan.
Sauté		the bananas only until they begin to brown lightly.
Place		on a cookie sheet pan with a spatula and bake at 350° for 5 minutes.
Serve		1 banana per guest in compote dishes topping each with
	3 Tbs.	SOUR CREAM sprinkled with
	1 Tbs.	BROWN SUGAR.

There are many variations which can be tried using the basic recipe above. Bananas may be dipped into the egg mixture, then in shredded coconut and baked for five minutes. Or you may use chopped peanuts instead of coconut. Or you may want to blend cracker crumbs with curry powder and cayenne pepper and proceed as above. All of these work well as accompaniments to any meat dish or may be used as dessert.

Ghana

ACCRA BANANA PEANUT CAKE

In a 2-quart bowl:

Sift	4 cups	ALL-PURPOSE FLOUR
	¼ cup	CAKE FLOUR
	4 tsp.	BAKING POWDER

	1 tsp.	SALT
	½ tsp.	BAKING SODA.

In a 3-quart bowl:

Cream	10 oz.	BUTTER OR MARGARINE with
	2 cups	SUGAR.
Blend in	4	EGGS lightly beaten.
Fold		the dry ingredients above alternately with
	8	MASHED BANANAS and
	½ cup	PEANUTS, coarsely chopped.
Bake		in a greased 9 × 12-inch baking pan at 350° for 30 minutes.
Test		with a toothpick. When toothpick comes out dry, cake is done.
Combine	½ cup	SUGAR with
	1 tsp.	CINNAMON.
Sprinkle		cake with cinnamon mixture as cake comes out of the oven.

Africa

MANGO-BANANA SUNDAE

Yield: 8 servings

Peel	1	MANGO and chop it finely.
Peel	2	BANANAS and chop them finely.
Combine		
Add	2 Tbs.	LEMON JUICE and
	½ cup	PINEAPPLE or ORANGE JUICE.
Place	1 scoop	VANILLA ICE CREAM in a sundae dish or sherbet glass.
Pour	3 to 4 Tbs.	MANGO-BANANA SAUCE over the ice cream. Serve.

BRANDIED APRICOT SUNDAE

Purée 2 cups   STEWED APRICOTS. Drain the liquid.

Add ½ cup   SUGAR
      ¼ cup   APRICOT BRANDY or COGNAC.

**Serve as
above.**

Liberia

MONROVIAN COCONUT PIE

This Monrovian pie is not a custard pie—it is made primarily of coconut, which absorbs the milk and eggs. Use fresh coconut if possible and grate it into long shreds. You haven't really tasted coconut pie until you've tried this one!

Yield: one 9-inch pie

Line a 9-inch pie pan with PIE CRUST. (Follow directions for packaged pie crust.)

Bake the pie shell for 5 minutes or until partially brown.

In a 3-quart bowl:

Cream 6 oz.   BUTTER (use 1½ 4-oz. sticks) with
      ½ cup   SUGAR until smooth.

Add 2   LARGE EGGS well beaten, and blend together.

Add 2 cups   GRATED COCONUT (if packaged, use moist)
      1 cup   MILK
      1 tsp.   VANILLA
      ¼ tsp.   BAKING SODA.

Pour into partially baked pie shell.

Cover the top with strips of crust in two directions.

Flute the edges.

Bake at 350° for 40 minutes or until golden brown.

Senegal

CARAMEL BANANAS

In a small skillet:

Heat	½ cup	WHITE SUGAR
	1 cup	LIGHT BROWN SUGAR
	3 Tbs.	EVAPORATED MILK
	2 Tbs.	BUTTER.
Cook	until sugar caramelizes (i.e., melts and starts to turn brown).	
Stir in	2 oz.	WHITE RUM and cool.
Slice	4	BANANAS.
Arrange	½	BANANA per person in compote dish.
Spoon	3 to 4 Tbs.	CARAMEL SAUCE over bananas.
Sprinkle	1 to 2 tsp.	CHOPPED PEANUTS over caramel sauce.

Rhodesia

PASSION FRUIT BAVARIAN CREAM

Passion-fruit juice may be obtained in gourmet food and specialty shops. If not available, use apricot nectar.

Dissolve	1 7½-oz. package	ORANGE GELATIN DESSERT in
	1½ cups	BOILING WATER.
Add	2 cups	PASSION-FRUIT JUICE.
Chill	until mixture begins to set. Stir well.	
Whip	1 cup	HEAVY CREAM until stiff.
Fold	whipped cream into the partially stiffened gelatine.	
Pile	lightly into wine glasses.	
Decorate	with a mound of toasted coconut in center of each dessert.	

Congo

PEANUT MOUSSE

Yield: 8 1½-cup portions

Dissolve	1 package (3¾ oz.) 2 cups	LEMON-FLAVORED GELATIN HOT WATER.
Blend in	½ cup	PEANUT BUTTER.
Fold in	6 1 cup	EGG WHITES beaten stiff and WHIPPED CREAM.
Pour	into stemmed glasses and chill.	
Place	2 Tbs.	WHIPPED CREAM on the mousse.
Top each with	1 tsp.	CHOCOLATE SPRINKLES or CHOCOLATE SHAVINGS.

Liberia

TROPICAL WHIP

There is no end to the variety of Tropical Whips you can make using different fruits in different combinations. Use the same proportions as in this recipe and you will have a lovely dessert. We found this particular recipe in Liberia but they are equally as popular in East and South Africa.

Yield: 8 portions

In an electric blender or mixer:

Beat	4 ¼ cup	EGG YOLKS with SUGAR until light.
Add	4 2 cups 1 cup ½ cup	MASHED BANANAS CRUSHED Pineapple (16-oz. can) ORANGE JUICE SHREDDED COCONUT.

Pour   into freezer pans and freeze until mushy.

Beat   4   EGG WHITES until stiff.

Add   ¼ cup   SUGAR.

Beat   to meringue consistency.

Fold   into fruits, and freeze until firm.

Serve   in dessert (or stemmed bar) glasses topped with

WHIPPED CREAM and
MARASCHINO CHERRIES with stems.

Uganda

KASHATA NA NAZI | Coconut Candy

Yield: 1½ lbs.

In a medium-sized heavy iron skillet:

Melt   2 cups   SUGAR stirring constantly until it is melted.

While the sugar is still white:

Add   2 cups   MOIST COCONUT (canned)
    1 tsp.   CINNAMON
    ½ tsp.   SALT.

Stir   hard for about 30 seconds.

Pour   into a 12 × 9-inch pan which has been lined with waxed paper.

Cut   into 1½-inch squares or diamonds while still hot.

Cool   until the *Kashatas* are set.

GROUNDNUT KASHATAS may be made by following the directions above but using roasted unsalted peanuts, chopped or whole, instead of coconut. Or you may wish to use half peanuts and half coconut for GROUND-NUT AND COCONUT KASHATAS. In Tanzania *Kashatas* are a great favorite in the market place and in Tanzanian homes they are served at tea time instead of cakes or cookies.

Ghana

BANANAS GHANA

Yield: 8 portions

Cut	8 medium	BANANAS in half lengthwise and then crosswise.
Blend	¼ cup	SUGAR and
	1 tsp.	CINNAMON and
Dip	the bananas in this mixture until coated.	
Place	the four quarters cut side down, side by side, in a 9-inch round or square ovenproof dish.	
Blend	1 cup	ORANGE JUICE with
	3 Tbs.	CURAÇAO or APRICOT BRANDY.
Pour	juice over all the bananas.	
Bake	at 350° for 20 minutes, basting with the juice if required.	
Sprinkle	4 Tbs.	SHREDDED COCONUT or CHOPPED PEANUTS over the top.
Serve	piping hot directly from baking dish.	
Pass	a bowl of	SWEETENED SOUR CREAM (use brown sugar) as a garnish.

Congo

SWEET ORANGES CONGO

Yield: 8 portions

Peel	4	CALIFORNIA ORANGES (thick skinned), cut in 1-inch slices then in ½-inch squares.
Add	1 cup	CHOPPED DATES
	½ cup	CHOPPED PEANUTS
	⅓ cup	APRICOT BRANDY or CURAÇAO.
Blend	all together.	
Divide	1 cup	MOIST SHREDDED COCONUT into 8 dessert sauce dishes (2 Tbs. or 1 oz. each).

Make a hole in the center of the coconut so that it forms a rim.

Fill centers with ORANGES CONGO, dividing above mixture evenly.

Add more brandy or orange juice if the mixture is not moist enough.

If you need a dessert in a hurry, prepare this dessert with canned mandarin oranges.

Another variation is to stuff baked apples with the above mixture when they are about half done.

Kenya

BRANDY SNAPS

Brandy Snaps are sensational cookies, originally introduced by the British. Never have we tasted Brandy Snaps like those made by the chef of the Outspan Hotel! Since the Nyerian chef makes 100 at a time, we cut his recipe down by three-quarters. However, after you make them once or twice, you may be making them 100 at a time, too.

Yield: 25 brandy snaps

In a pot:

Combine	4 oz.	BUTTER
	½ cup	SUGAR
	½ cup	CORN SYRUP
	½ tsp.	GROUND GINGER.

Stir over heat until well mixed.

Cool for 10 minutes.

Add ⅓ cup   ALL-PURPOSE FLOUR and blend into mixture.

Pour mixture by spoonfuls into flat greased pan 3 to 4 inches apart.

Bake at 350° until snaps flatten.

Remove carefully with spatula and, when slightly cooled,

Roll up into a tube.

Combine	3 Tbs.	BRANDY with
	1 pint	WHIPPED CREAM.

Stuff tubes with whipped cream using a pastry bag.

PAWPAW PARADISE

You really should use papaya for this drink, but mangos will provide a good substitute if papayas are not available.

Peel	1 ripe papaya.	
Cut	in small pieces and purée in electric blender.	
Add	½ cup	MILK
	1 cup	DARK RUM
	1 cup	CRUSHED ICE
	2 Tbs.	SUGAR.
Blend	until thoroughly smooth.	
Pour into	4-ounce glasses.	
Garnish with	1	STRAWBERRY each.

WHITE ELEPHANT

In a blender:

Combine	1 cup	MOIST SHREDDED COCONUT (canned) or fresh
	1 cup	MILK (use coconut milk if available)
	4 Tbs.	SUGAR
	6 oz.	WHITE RUM
	2 oz.	WHITE CRÈME DE CACAO
	1 cup	CRUSHED ICE.
Mix	until smooth and thick.	
Pour	into 4-ounce glasses.	
Sprinkle with		SHREDDED COCONUT as a garnish.
Serve	with a straw.	

PINEAPPLE BUGANDA

Yield: 1 quart

In a blender:

Combine 2 cups   FRESH PINEAPPLE, very ripe and cut in small pieces.
          4 Tbs.   BROWN SUGAR
          ½ cup   LIGHT CREAM (or milk)
          6 oz.   WHITE RUM
          1 tsp.   VANILLA EXTRACT
          1 cup   CRUSHED ICE.

Blend   until smooth and thick.

Serve with   MINT SPRIGS and a MARASCHINO CHERRY in whiskey-sour glasses.

ETHIOPIAN PUNCH (nonalcoholic)

Yield: 1 gallon

In a punch bowl:

Combine 1 cup   RASPBERRY SYRUP
          1 cup   MARASCHINO-CHERRY JUICE
          1 cup   ORANGE JUICE
          1 cup   LEMON JUICE
          1 cup   PINEAPPLE JUICE
          1 cup   GRAPE JUICE
          2½ quarts   WATER, SPARKLING WATER or 7-UP.

Serve   out of punch bowl with plenty of ice.

Garnish with   ORANGE SLICES.

JUNGLE FLAME

Yield: 3 cups

Combine: 1 cup   LIME SYRUP
          1 cup   LEMON JUICE
          1 cup   WHITE RUM.

Shake   with ice.

Strain   into whiskey sour glasses.

Garnish   with twists of lemon.

SENEGALI SUNSHINE

Yield: 1 quart plus

Peel   1   CALIFORNIA (thick-skinned) ORANGE rind very thinly and close to the edge, avoiding the white pulp, and chop finely.

Place   the rind in the blender with

2 cups	ORANGE JUICE
6 oz.	WHITE RUM
2 oz.	CURAÇAO
4 oz.	LIGHT CREAM
1 cup	CRUSHED ICE.

Blend   until thoroughly smooth and thick.

Pour   into 4-ounce glasses.

Garnish with   ORANGE SLICES and FRESH STRAWBERRIES.

TANZANIAN TONIC

Yield: 1 quart plus

In a blender:

Combine	1 cup	PINEAPPLE JUICE
	1 cup	PAPAYA (or Apricot) NECTAR
	1 cup	GUAVA (or Peach) NECTAR
	2 oz.	LEMON JUICE
	2 oz.	ORANGE JUICE
	1 oz.	GRENADINE
	6 oz.	LIGHT RUM.

Blend   until smooth.

Pour   over ice in 4-oz. glasses, adding a dash of dark rum as it is served.

Garnish with   HALVED ORANGE SLICES and STEMMED MARASCHINO CHERRIES.

Appendix

All About Coconut

Preparing Grated Fresh Coconut

Pierce two holes in the "eyes"—the shiny black marks on the coconut.

Drain the water from the coconut.

Break the coconut with a sharp blow from a hammer into two or three pieces.

Place a small amount of water into each of the pieces so that the meat will come away from the shell easily.

Bake pieces in the oven at 325° for five minutes.

Pare the rind of coconut with swivel-type vegetable peeler.

Grate by hand or cut in small chunks and chop in an electric blender.

Toasted Coconut

Spread the shredded coconut evenly over a cookie sheet and bake at 325° for about ten minutes. In Africa, coconut is only toasted when used as an accompaniment to curry.

How to Prepare Coconut Liquids

Our cookbook refers to three kinds of coconut liquids:

Coconut Water

The liquid inside a fresh coconut. This liquid is *not* coconut milk, as is commonly believed. It is actually almost pure water. When using fresh coconut in a recipe, always use the coconut water as part of the liquid in making the sauce or add to the water required in the recipe.

Coconut Milk

The liquid extracted when hot water is poured over grated coconut, whether fresh or packaged. Here is how to make it.

Place	2 cups	GRATED COCONUT in a cheesecloth in a sieve over a bowl.
Pour	1 cup	BOILING WATER over coconut and, when cool enough,
Squeeze		the coconut as dry as possible.
Pour	1 cup	BOILING WATER over coconut again and repeat process.

Coconut Cream

This is the liquid extracted when *hot milk* is poured over grated coconut, whether fresh or packaged. To make it, use the same method as for Coconut Milk but use hot milk instead of water.

Prepared Coconut Commercially Available

MOIST COCONUT is available grated, flaked, or shredded in packages or cans. DRY COCONUT is usually packaged. In using dry coconut for coconut milk and cream, use ⅓ cup extra for every cup called for. POWDERED COCONUT is available in gourmet shops and better food markets. This also may be used in making Coconut Milk or Coconut Cream as indicated on package.

How to Prepare Seasoned Butters

Purified Butter Ethiopian Style

In Ethiopia, every housewife keeps seasoned butter, called *ghee,* in her refrigerator or in a cool place ready for use. The Ethiopians believe that the addition of spices and herbs actually purifies the butter. This is how it is made.

Sauté	¼ cup	SCALLIONS, finely chopped
	2 cloves	GARLIC, mashed
	1 small piece	GINGER, chopped, in
	1 lb.	BUTTER
		on a low fire until butter starts to boil.
Add	1 tsp.	GROUND CLOVES
	1 tsp.	GROUND CINNAMON
	1 tsp.	TURMERIC
	½ tsp.	CARDAMOM SEEDS.

Simmer gently for about 5 minutes but do not permit butter to brown.

Strain through a double cheesecloth.

Store in a crock in the refrigerator and spoon over vegetables, etc.

Seasoned Butter American Style

Here is a secret method used in many American restaurants. The butter is kept in the refrigerator at all times ready for use in seasoning soups, sauces, vegetables and meats, fish and poultry.

Soften	1 lb.	BUTTER and
	1 lb.	MARGARINE.
Blend in	2 Tbs.	SALT
	½ tsp.	BLACK PEPPER
	1 tsp.	ONION POWDER
	1 tsp.	GARLIC POWDER
	1 tsp.	PAPRIKA
	⅛ tsp.	OREGANO or THYME.

Place   the softened butter in a crock and spoon it out as you use it. There is generally no further need to season.

All About Greens

There are those who believe that greens should always be torn, but in the restaurant industry there is no time for tearing and I have found that I prefer the cut greens even when time is no problem. The fibers are not so delicate that proper handling and cutting with a knife will injure them and they look more attractive. They should be cut as close to the time of use as possible.

Preparing Greens

For greens with loose leaves such as BOSTON, SIMPSON LETTUCE, ROMAINE, CHICORY and ESCAROLE use the following procedure:

Remove   wilted greens and wash the outside in *lukewarm* water.

Cut   across the head one inch from the core and discard the core.

Fill   sink partly full of lukewarm water and toss a handful of coarse salt (kosher) into the water.

Loosen   the leaves, wash thoroughly, and rinse.

Set   desired leaves for salad liners aside on a turkish towel to dry.

For tight leaf lettuce such as ICEBERG:

Remove   wilted greens and wash outside in *lukewarm* water.

Set   aside good outside leaves for tossed greens.

Cut   out core with the point of a paring knife.

Cut   the head down from the core into two equal halves.

Hold   the halves, one in each hand cut side up, and allow lukewarm water from the faucet to run through the leaves.

Turn   upside down and drain on a dry turkish towel.

Pat   the leaves dry.

The flat outer leaves of a lettuce head are good for lining salad bowls and for sandwiches. The inner leaves or core, may be cut into thin julienne strips and used like cole slaw. Grate the core into your tossed salad.

Greens for Tossing

Take   as many leaves in left hand as you can, lay them across board.

Slice   across with stainless steel French knife in 1-inch strips. (If the strips are too long cut them in desired lengths.)

Pat   the leaves dry with a towel.

Lift   the leaves about 12 inches high and drop them loosely into a bowl or container. This aerates the greens.

Making a Lettuce Cup

Use   ICEBERG LETTUCE.

Turn   lettuce cut side up after the head was cut in halves.

Tap   it lightly with the side of your fist to loosen the leaves, taking care not to break them. Outside leaves will come out as cups.

Form   a cup with two or three leaves with the *cut side out* so that the edges of the salads are uniform and clean looking. The larger outer leaves are for entrée salads. The smaller cups may be used for side dishes or small side salads.

How to Cut Onions

On our visit to Africa we were very fortunate in having the opportunity to actually help in preparing meals with many African women. On these occasions my contribution was usually a demonstration of short-cut techniques. The ladies were delighted and particularly impressed with how we handle onions. It was their idea that I describe the technique in this book.

This method was taught to me by an old-time chef who once said, "I can run any kitchen with four tools: a French knife, a paring knife, a mixing spoon and a wire whisk.'' (I would add the swivel-type vegetable peeler and perhaps a few more, but the important point is to start with the right tools.) Beginning with the indispensable French knife, his technique is as follows.

Cut   the onions in half.

Trim   the skin and cut away the core.

Place   it *cut side down* on a wooden board.

Make   three diagonal gashes on each side across the onion.

Hold   onion on the board cut side down with thumb and fingers around the onion.

Slice   down as thinly or thickly as desired, leaving slices in place.

Swing   the onion around and slice down again.

Spread   onions over the board.

Hold   point of the French knife in left hand and handle of knife in the right hand.

Chop   the onions by holding the point of the knife on the board and bringing the blade and handle up and down without moving the point.

Today onions may be purchased as onion powder, onion salt, onion flakes, frozen in packages, and even freeze-dried. All are good. But somehow it's hard to find a substitute for good old onions that make you weep.

Accompaniments for Curry

Curries are almost as popular throughout Africa as they are in India. The curry of Africa, however, is not like the Madras blend. It is bright orange in color and has a most distinctive flavor. Accompaniments are as important in the service of curries in Africa as elsewhere. The following are suggested for an African Curry.

Chutney   Mango Chutney is usually purchased ready-made in Africa. But the housewives in ''Curry Territory'' make wonderful chutney. See Pineapple Chutney, page 192. They also make plum chutney, lime pickle, and green tomato and ripe tomato chutneys.

Fruits   Chopped bananas sprinkled with lime juice.
Chopped bananas, melon, mango, or papaya.
Lime wedges.

Vegetables   Skinned and chopped tomatoes in equal parts with black raisins.
Chopped scallions mixed with hard-boiled eggs.
Batter-fried onion rings.
Sautéed onions.
Chopped onions with green peppers.

Nuts   Coconut, grated, shredded, toasted.
Peanuts, whole or chopped.
Cashew nuts.

Six accompaniments are adequate for a curry dish. Prepare about ½ cup of each and place them in small bowls or in a six-sectioned relish dish.

African Artifacts

How to Make African Salad Bowls

Small salads were served in coconut bowls throughout West Africa. They are simply made as follows:

Cut   the coconut across in two equal halves with an electric meat saw or prevail upon your butcher to do this for you. (If you wish you may remove the liquid first and use the unscarred half only.)

Place   in oven at 325° until meat comes cleanly away from shell.

Sandpaper   the outside of the bowl until glossy smooth.

How to Make an African Coconut Ladle

An African coconut ladle is a surprisingly handy item to have around the house and is especially appropriate to use when you serve your African dinner.

Pierce	two holes in the "eyes" or black dots at the peak of the coconut, with an ice pick or sharp skewer.
Drain	the water.
Cut	the coconut in two making the peak end the smaller half. This half is discarded. (Have your butcher cut the coconut on his electric meat saw.)
Place	the coconut in the oven at 325° until the meat comes cleanly away from the shell.
Bore	a "tight" ½-inch hole on the side of the half without the shiny dots—about ¾ inch from the edge with an electric bit.
Force	a 12-inch-long dowel stick ½ inch thick through the hole in the coconut, so that it comes through ½ inch on the inside of the ladle. (Purchase the dowel stick at the carpentry shop.)
Sandpaper	the outside of your new ladle until it is glossy smooth.